FRO N
REAL CLEAN

How to Create A Fully Functional
Relationship With Your Teenager

VANESSA BAKER

BALBOA.PRESS
A DIVISION OF HAY HOUSE

This book is a work of non-fiction. Unless otherwise noted, the author and the publisher make no explicit guarantees as to the accuracy of the information contained in this book and in some cases, names of people and places have been altered to protect their privacy.

Balboa Press books may be ordered through booksellers or by contacting:

Balboa Press
A Division of Hay House
1663 Liberty Drive
Bloomington, IN 47403
www.balboapress.com
844-682-1282

Because of the dynamic nature of the Internet, any web addresses or links contained in this book may have changed since publication and may no longer be valid. The views expressed in this work are solely those of the author and do not necessarily reflect the views of the publisher, and the publisher hereby disclaims any responsibility for them.

The author of this book does not dispense medical advice or prescribe the use of any technique as a form of treatment for physical, emotional, or medical problems without the advice of a physician, either directly or indirectly. The intent of the author is only to offer information of a general nature to help you in your quest for emotional and spiritual well-being. In the event you use any of the information in this book for yourself, which is your constitutional right, the author and the publisher assume no responsibility for your actions.

Any people depicted in stock imagery provided by Getty Images are models, and such images are being used for illustrative purposes only. Certain stock imagery © Getty Images.

Print information available on the last page.

ISBN: 978-1-9822-6233-4 (sc)
ISBN: 978-1-9822-6235-8 (hc)
ISBN: 978-1-9822-6234-1 (e)

Library of Congress Control Number: 2021901220

Balboa Press rev. date: 01/15/2021

Contents

Preface

Raising happy, healthy teenagers who turn into kind and responsible adults while maintaining (and even increasing) our own happiness and health is possible. My entire life is about exactly that.

Between August 2002 and January 2008, I gave birth to five babies. When they were two, three, five, six, and eight years old, I remember thinking, *You know what this means, Vanessa? In ten years, they're going to be twelve, thirteen, fifteen, sixteen, and eighteen!*

I'm doomed, according to—well, *everyone!* I can't think of a single person who was able to express any type of hope or encouragement for me, the mother of five future simultaneous teenagers. Not in my family, not at church, not at school, not at the grocery store, at the mall, on Facebook, at the park—nowhere. It was just like how you spy a huge zit on the end of someone's nose and think, *Oh man, that's gonna be very nasty very soon.* But I heard all those thoughts out loud from everyone, every day—and when I say *every day*, I mean it.

As I write this, my children are exactly those "dreaded" ages, from twelve to eighteen, and while I wouldn't describe parenting them as easy, I can confirm that I didn't drink the punch—and we are not doomed.

I was not going to go down like that. It was a do-or-die type of resolve that took over my mind and heart ten years ago. A few years later, I heard Dr. Brené Brown say that she told her husband that she intended to start a worldwide conversation about shame and courage. It didn't sound like a super-sexy or particularly great idea that had a chance of catching on, but she knew it was a conversation that needed to happen, so she totally went for it. (If you're not already familiar with the breadth and depth and quality of the shift she has caused in humanity, please get to know her work.)

This book is one calculated aspect of a multifront attack I'm executing on the old way of thinking about parenting teenagers. See, I'm already calling it the "old way" of thinking.

This mighty little book is my totally going for it on fulfilling my mission: to be courageous and free to be, do, and say the exact thing that will move you and your teenager from pain to healing, from hate to love, from control to trust, and from fear to full self-expression so that you both can live out the joy and power of being who you both were made to be.

The intricacy of my past, from my own childhood up to just yesterday, all of my experiences and failures, observations, education, and development have led me to this moment in my life.

I can tell you, wholeheartedly and without a shred of doubt, that my life's work is dedicated to something that many people may call a lost cause: creating solid, clean, real relationships with teenagers. I can teach you to create a relationship in which you can be who you are, not some "parent-y" version of yourself who you never wanted to become. I also can show you how to sustain and enjoy a relationship with your teen that works, regardless of past, experiences, personalities, or "impossible" circumstances.

Even if your kids are adults now or are a year away from moving out, this book can make an important difference in your experience of life from here on out.

If your kids are little and you're being proactive, this book can make an important difference in your experience of life from here on out.

You have done a very smart thing in picking up this book. You should thank the person who recommended this book to you. I will not let you down, but I'm going to need you to dig in. Reading this book isn't a casual situation. This isn't a pick-and-choose-your-chapters type of thing. It's one whole—and the parts *do not* equal the whole. They'll be nice little tidbits if you dabble in this text, but my design is deliberate and exact. If you read this book as if your teen's happiness and health—and your own happiness and health—depend upon it, you will cause the breakthrough that you want.

Let's go. It's time to challenge yourself in ways that your teenager might only dream of.

Introduction

It doesn't have to be so hard, but I know why it is. The overwhelmingly common message we hear from random strangers when they see we're expecting or they see our smiling toddlers riding upon our shoulders at the park is, "Wait until they're teenagers! Enjoy them while you can—before they become insufferable know-it-alls who only care about themselves and who quit talking to you!"

Then, our own parents may perpetuate the message—the "truth" about what it's like to raise teenagers (namely, what it was like to raise *us*). It's hard not to buy into this rhetoric, but when a problem is accepted as *the way it is*, then we naturally think it's unavoidable; we don't think there's anything we can do about it.

If the auto mechanic told you that your dream car was not worth fixing, that it was beyond repair, you'd walk away and cut your losses. It would suck, but you likely wouldn't attempt to recover something that a trusted expert said could not be repaired.

Now, multiply the way some people love their cars by the infinite, hopeless love you (may have) felt when you laid eyes on your baby. If it fits better, think about the intense sense of pressure and responsibility you have for the well-being of that baby. This is not a simple undertaking, for as much as we desperately want to do it right—to be respected and remembered by our kids as being a great parent who is/was loving, fair, wise, and a positive influence in their lives—it may be useful to admit that, on some level, we have either given up or made ourselves or our teenagers into the bad guy because it's not going very well, and we're out of ideas!

I happen to have some really effective and simple-at-their-core kind of ideas for you. Stick with me. I'll never judge you, shame you, or blame you. As teachers often do, I'll put words to what you know in your gut feels right, and I'll hit the pause button to show you where you may have gotten off track.

We will explore what MEAN, REAL, and CLEAN stand for and why they matter. We will look at what a fully functioning relationship sounds like, looks like, and feels like.

Listen—don't freak out if you only bought this book and didn't know I also have a course titled "From MEAN to REAL CLEAN: How to Create a Fully Functional Relationship with Your Teen in Five Steps." The five steps set the course apart from this book.

This book stands alone. Reading it and applying it will serve you well as you alter your mindset on parenting your teenager. As you know, there are other ways to learn and apply new information besides reading a book. There also are opportunities to go deeper in any knowledge set.

In the course, I teach the acronyms MEAN, REAL, and CLEAN and what a fully functional relationship is like. I go into more detail in this book than I do in the course. In fact, this book is a part of that course. I created an interactive workbook. I support you on Facebook in my private group. I offer additional content, group coaching, challenges, etc., to keep you in this mindset and to continue to deepen and strengthen my teachings.

In the course, I've added a second half, which is the five-steps part. It's very challenging, very deep, very difficult. It's the work that will cement the MEAN, REAL, and CLEAN concepts into your life. You will be trained and held to account. You will change. When you have completed the five steps, you will not be the same, and neither will your teenagers or your relationship with them.

It's a big deal. It's expensive. It's time-consuming, and you will get your entire life out of it. It's priceless too. You might wish you could pay me ten more payments when you're done!

This book isn't a commercial for something else, but it is part of something that is also very powerful in its own right.

Part 1
MEAN

It's not the *mean* you might think. It's not the one where you intend to harm another. The kind of *mean* that parents may feel they are or are told they are is different. Let me break it down. MEAN is an acronym you can use when you're not feeling like yourself.

Misunderstood
Entitled
Authoritative
Numb

Misunderstood

You're Only Human

When our lives are stressful due to unworkable relationships, job expectations, finances, or health issues, it is very common for us to under-communicate with our teens about what is going on in our lives. We don't need to share every detail; we just need to tell them that we're in a hard spot and are working on finding a solution. When we're stressed, we sometimes want to pretend we aren't struggling at all, but that isn't the truth, so our stress comes out sideways. It's very natural for us to take out our frustration and stress on the people around us, like our teenagers, when it isn't about them. Because they don't know yet what it's like to be an adult, they often assume that it's their fault we are having a hard time.

Here's a counterexample: Imagine you just closed a deal, got a raise, or were publicly praised in a meeting by a client or your boss. You go home and see the same dishes on the coffee table and the same smelly kids sitting on the same couch, but since you're feeling happy, proud, and extra great about yourself, you somehow overlook the very things that normally would set you off. You handle yourself differently. It's easier to access your kindness and to have better interactions.

Too bad life's not like that every day. It's more likely that you're tired, dehydrated, hungry, worn out, sad, frustrated, or overwhelmed, and the way that you react or respond is "mean." But, really, you're just being a human who needs a break, a sandwich, a nap, a little help. It can be difficult to bridge the gap between feeling an emotion and expressing it to your teenager.

Example: Your teen asks to go somewhere, to buy something, then starts to complain, and you just snap! You might even blame them or overreact about something pretty benign because of your own situation. They bark back. Then you. Then them. It's over and you realize (maybe) that they were just your scapegoat.

Imagine saying, "It's not you. I'm just totally worn out right now. Can you come back in twenty minutes, and I'll give you my full attention?" Then you handle yourself and resume. Mindfully, reasonably. You still can say no to whatever they needed or wanted, still help them if they were being out of line, but you'll do it from a place of clarity rather than reaction.

What if the reasons you are feeling like a failure or extra frustrated in your role with your teenager is so simple? What if …? And if this is all you've got going on, I hope you kept your receipt for this book! Take it back and get a refund, ASAP!

What if you're not who you want to be for your teenager because you have been terrible about taking care of yourself?

Imagine getting three good meals and some snacks, being

hydrated, not staying up too late, getting some fun and relaxation in your life, asking for the help you need in all the areas of your life—imagine fighting for it! Imagine enjoying nature, friends, naps, books, and stretching. What if this "mean" version of you that's showing up is just the neglected you who is grumpy as hell about being ignored?

What do you need? Don't say *nothing*. Do not even start with me. You are a human. You are a human under pressure. You may deprive yourself when you are stressed. You may believe there is no possibility for you to meet your needs because you have too much responsibility or you lack time, money, support, or even judgment, but I call bullshit.

You may indulge yourself instead of depriving yourself. Even so, you're still masking your real needs by piling on a bunch of short-term feel-good moments. These can look like any kind of mind-altering escape route, numbing substance, or behavior, such as shopping, cleaning, eating, drinking, drugs, sex, porn, TV, social media, drama, or altering your physical appearance. There are so many things in which to indulge yourself, but you're still depriving yourself of what you need, hoping the real need will go away.

Here's how I know you're full of it: if your friends were running themselves into the ground or just checking out of their lives, you'd see it, you'd say something, and you'd help them. You'd even sacrifice to make sure their needs were met, that they could sustain and thrive in their lives. You would. I know you would. So now I need you to show up like *that*—for *you*.

What if the reason you sometimes or often feel like a "mean" parent is because you're actually oozing out the meanness that is always brewing inside of you? What are the chances that you'd be gentler, more thoughtful, and more measured in your approach to parenting if you were treating yourself as a live person and not a machine? (No offense if you're actually a robot.)

Let's Talk about Communication

Even when two parties intend to have clear, effective communication, it can be difficult, so imagine if one of the parties is yelling or nagging, and the other is yelling back or ignoring them or doesn't have much to say for themselves. This makes for misunderstandings. I think all of us felt misunderstood, to some degree, as teenagers, but I am going to make the case that parents are misunderstood to an unworkable degree. Here's why:

When we meet our little babies for the first time, we are sure that all we want is for our kids to be happy, to grow up and be able to navigate the world, to support themselves or get the support they need. When we are faced with who our babies become a decade and a half later, we would settle for them getting their wet towel off the floor or waking up on time for once, for the love of God! We get reduced to policing agents who are on the lookout for signs of current annoyance and trends for future failure.

Our communication is then reduced to barking, pointing out flaws and mistakes, lecturing, and preaching to a congregation of one uninterested audience member. Sometimes we just can't get through, and we are misunderstood and called "mean" or worse, when we just want them to be considerate, kind, responsible people.

Depending on how and if we were taught to communicate and our level of interest in coming to agreements versus just saying a bunch of things we think, communication can break down quickly. For some parents, volume and anger are the main avenues for trying to get through.

It's obvious to us, as parents, that we get frustrated because we care so much about the outcome of our kids' last few years at home and their ability to succeed in the future and to be enjoyable now. For teenagers, the anger, the nagging, the yelling, and the criticism is us trying to control them, not caring about what they need or want, or being "extra." They usually just decide that we just don't get it. We are hopeless.

Siri, play "Parents Just Don't Understand" by Will Smith. Luckily, this is fixable!

Mama/Papa Bear Mode

Sometimes, misunderstanding can also look like you just wanting them to be safe from the ten thousand threats that exist in our world, even when we are safe at home.

Example: Your teen wants something, to branch out or make plans, and you shut it down because while you want them to grow and be happy, you have more concerns than you can process. So it's a *no*. That's it. You're the parent. No conversation.

Your heart is in the right place; you just couldn't handle the risk. They get mad and maybe do it anyway. You feel out of control. They think you don't care or listen—"mean."

Whether you call it helicopter parenting or mama/papa-bear parenting, if you look closely at it, we are reducing a kid's opportunity to learn things the hard way, to get hurt, and to then recover, grow stronger, and become resilient. This type of overprotection is not just viewed as mean or unreasonable by our kids, but it also actually stunts their growth by actively preventing their failure.

We want kids who are confident and self-assured, strong, and able to bounce back. The only way that they can become that is if we extend their boundaries—max them out, even—to the safest point that they can handle. I say "max them out" because isn't that how you've grown, every time? Being pushed to a limit, being uncomfortable, and then rising up with a new sense of what you can handle and navigate in life?

Maybe you believe your teen doesn't deserve the right to push their limits, to try to grow, because they messed it up last time, but that is the exact reason to allow for more opportunities to learn. Why do we expect our teens to nail it because we were sure we explained a challenge thoroughly? Lessons are usually learned through experience, not preaching and protecting.

I can tell you honestly that, in the past few years, I learned many of the lessons I have been trying to teach my teenagers. Self-care is one. Self-love is another. I am in my forties! I am just now truly understanding some of the principles that I pretended I had worked out for myself or pretended applied to everyone but me. So we have to step back, calm down, and let it sink in that there are no shortcuts to growing and learning in this life. It's a very annoying and never-ending endeavor sometimes, for them and for us!

Overreacting

There are many times when we, as parents, time-travel far into the future when we notice our kids have a certain habit, tendency or behavior, and we react (internally and externally) to fears that may or may not come to pass. This is part of our role as protector—to see the danger and pain that could be ahead for our kids and to help them to avoid that, whether or not they understand or like it.

With teenagers, though, we have to take into account that they may have a great capacity and ability to weigh their own options and then handle themselves in a worst-case scenario.

When we just shut down their ideas, we block an opportunity to teach them how to make mindful decisions based on multiple factors. When we are biased, fear-based, or coming from our own past traumas, we make their opportunity to think and learn less of the focus than it needs to be.

Our true desire and a long-term win are probably more in line with managing our own emotions, triggers, and concerns and creating a space to have a conversation that promotes thorough consideration—not just on your part but also modeling it for them. Your teen may or may not come to the same conclusion as you do, but in your resisting overreaction, you may get to see something new that you couldn't see before—and it's likely that they will too.

The win here is to remove the heat from the conversation, the fight-or-flight feeling that drives you to overreact, and to allow space for the subject at hand to be the issue, not the emotions and subsequent defense that they breed, which can lead to a shutdown and little to no growth or learning.

By the way, I'd like to point out the irony of our freaking out in defense and anger when someone tells us we are overreacting. Or instead, employing a freaky steel-faced, eyes-glazed-over response that has us seem in control and reacting "calmly," but is even scarier than the anger.

Assumptions

Parents with whom I work often admit they have no idea what they are doing, and they feel outmatched by their teenagers. They do not know how to win or how to make the kind of difference they want to make with their kids. No matter how successful or together they might be in other areas of their lives, like career or health or other relationships, they feel inadequate to handle this phase of parenting.

As a result of feeling out of control at times, it is normal to grasp assumptions because they can feel like a life raft in the rapids. It's tricky because when we make assumptions, we often see them as the truth so it doesn't occur to us that they are assumptions.

As my dad always said, if you assume, you make an "ass" out of "u" and "me." Silly, but true. We think the worst of our teenagers, and then they are offended. We defend our assumptions, based on our past experiences and knowledge. Then, we either fight to the death, or they shut down, or both! Game over.

We, as parents, need to be more curious and interested in what is actually the case, instead of jumping to conclusions. We may jump to conclusions because we hold on to any certainty we can find. It's understandable, and I have compassion for us on that. I hope you do too.

The problem is that we don't learn anything new. We don't have any option or space to collect clues and valuable insights and nuances that would help us truly understand what our teen is dealing with, reacting to, and worried or angry about.

Parents I worked with assumed that their teenager was lazy, didn't care about school, and wanted a free ride. They built up a complete character in their minds that wasn't at all accurate. They just saw her grades. *She has C's. She is smart; she should have A's. She is lazy. She is on her phone too much.*

When I got to talk with her, I realized quickly that she did want to do well, but she was dealing with a lot of social stress that was impacting her ability to focus and perform as well as she used to do. In addition, she had been in a gifted program in middle school, but now that she was in high school, she wasn't sheltered in that small world, where everything seemed to come easily. She was no longer favored or special in her mind, as she was now in mainstream classes. We realized quickly that she hadn't learned resiliency. She hadn't learned how to struggle and prevail. I could go on and on, but I'll point out the obvious: She was not lazy. She is and was a complex human being who was affected by multiple factors. She needed support, not judgment based on assumptions.

She misunderstood her parents' response. Their assessment of her was based on their theory that if they got her motivated and taught her to "stop being lazy," then she would get all A's. So they controlled, they yelled, they took away her freedom, and they nagged. They were "mean," and she did not get the help she needed from them. They just wanted her to feel good about herself and achieve to her potential.

When we misjudge/misunderstand the situation at hand because we already know what's going on, we don't even think to get curious and interested, and then, we respond in a way that invites confusion and further disagreement and upset. It's a mess!

Future Implications of Being Misunderstood

Being misunderstood is often a by-product of choosing to not understand in the first place. It's a chain reaction, and it doesn't matter whose fault it is; the end result is the same. You aren't understood, and they aren't either. Naturally, that is a primary cause of breakdowns in a relationship, as relationships are based on mutual understanding and respect.

If we don't handle this very common state of affairs intentionally, there is a strong chance that, ten years into the future, lack of common ground, poor listening, and misunderstandings will have compounded. We are either left with a surface-level relationship or a tumultuous one. Either way, it's not happy or healthy, and we will look back and wish we had taken better care of ourselves so we could be our best for our teenagers during a difficult time of life. We will look back and regret not being more patient and open-minded, getting to the root of the issue, and accepting the reality of what our teens were dealing with or trying to tell us. We will look back and kick ourselves for overprotecting, overreacting, jumping to conclusions, and thinking we knew it all. We may experience some semblance of control in the moment, but the most-likely outcome when we don't go deeper when we are misunderstood won't be the outcome we were hoping for.

Entitled

Who? Me?

Entitled is an adjective we may reserve for "kids these days." But have you ever thought or said out loud the following statements?

- I am the adult. You have to respect me.
- I am the parent. I demand your attention and/or obedience.
- I pay the bills so you have to do what I say.

- I am lonely. You should want to hang out with me like when you were little. I'm your parent.
- I do so much for you. Why can't you lift a finger for me?

If so, you may have slipped into thinking that because of your role, you deserve certain privileges and honors. That would be so cool, but getting others (anyone!) to consistently and honestly desire to please you, regardless of your relationship (as opposed to your title or role) is not usually how it goes.

Think about a job you had in your younger days. The kid one grade above you gets promoted to assistant manager, and now you have to respect him—and it's like a free pass for him to torment and make demands of you. Those who are the most timid or spineless among us generally respond obediently to such superficial power dynamics. Yes, we certainly deserve more respect than the new assistant manager in this example, but it must be through trust and mutual respect that we are motivated to perform, not out of obligation and hierarchy.

Consider that you may get what you want when you're watching your inferiors, when they are within your earshot, but what is the truth about your relationship? Is there mutual respect? Is there a sense of cooperation? Kindness?

Consider also that it's the typical scenario in which kids are prone to look the part for show and then do what they want in secret.

The real question is, when you just deserve the relationship without working for it, does it work out?

Contention for Attention

Usually, it's when kids are around twelve or thirteen years old that their parents start feeling threatened by their kids' lack of interest in spending time with them, doing the types of activities and little traditions that they used to love. They stay in their rooms a lot more, say no to hanging out with the family, and seem to dread being a part of the normal activities. It is so easy to take this behavior personally, but if we don't realize that it is natural for young teenagers to start breaking off from the family, form their own identities, make closer friends, and want to be more independent, it can feel like a knife in the heart.

We must give them space and not insist that they "owe" us a certain amount of time or are required to be as they were in the previous stage of life. If we aren't careful, all of our interactions will be negative—a constant tug-of-war between what they need and what we need from them.

I am 100 percent for kids of all ages participating in the work of the home, the special moments, and whatever the family values as a group, but there is a danger in the relationship when we can't understand (or don't want to accept) that things are changing in our teens. The dynamic shifts, from our insisting on how things go to our being invited to participate in their lives, as they need us to.

Teens aren't normally able to communicate that they are changing, growing, and seeking more alone time, friend time, and independence, and they may even seem very rude when they are called out on this change. I've talked to teens who miss being little and are scared to be older, but they aren't sure how to handle this "in the middle" part. They feel terrible that their parents make them feel guilty and don't listen to their needs, their cues, and their requests for more privacy and space.

If we are clear as parents that no one—not even our own children—is obligated to be in our presence, then the wonderful irony is that they will be much more likely to want to be with us. This is because they know we are letting them lead. We are mature and wise enough to hang back and let them say what they need from the parent/child relationship. The biggest bonus of this approach is that when they do have questions and confusion, stress and trouble, they will come to us first. They will trust that we won't make whatever they are facing into a huge deal or make it about us (our fears and our own triggers from our own pasts, stories on the news, whatever our friends' kids are doing, and so on).

We need to find ways to fill up our hearts with love, attention, and connection in other ways than from our own teenagers. It's not their responsibility to keep us company, to fill our voids, or to distract us from our own loneliness or boredom. We have to get a life, if we haven't already, so we can genuinely celebrate that they are getting one too.

Agreement

A very common theme in my coaching practice is parents calling their teens disrespectful and accusing them of having bad attitudes or worse because they see the world in a different way than their parents do. This comes up in all kinds of areas: style choices, politics, worldviews, time-management strategies, food preferences, passions, causes, music genres, career interests, financial goals, and so on.

You may be able to see something here, if you look with a very humble attitude. Do you feel insulted or even surprised when your teenager takes up an interest or develops a point of view that does not align with your own? It may come out like a judgment or a negative comment about the diverging thought—a knee-jerk impulse to say no or say whatever uninformed ideas you may have about the new point of view, usually based on assumptions and not fully investigated with your teenager.

Sometimes, parents assume that their kids will be like them. Some parents have admitted to me that, deep down, they feel like they've done something wrong if their kids' values, interests, and preferences don't reflect those of the family. I hear a lot of, "In this family, we do this," or "In the house, we believe this, and we don't believe in that."

Of course, right or wrong, it's useful to have a firm stance on basic human-decency things, but when we say, "In this family," or "In this house," it would be more accurate to say, "I need everyone to think my way about things." There is no house or family standard that exists inherently. There are inherited norms, ideals, traditions, values, and preferences that may tend to be followed in multiple generations or from the oldest kid down to the youngest, but these inherited ideals, for a child who doesn't authentically feel the same way or share the same interests, may seem oppressive, inhibitive, and even tyrannical.

I have a client whose parents are very talented and accomplished athletes. They were clashing with their teenager because he didn't share their passion for sweat, pain, and competition. He loved music, art, and reading. They did too, as, of course, no one is one label or is that simple, but they insisted on having him go out for teams, work out all the time, go to coaching sessions, and get private trainers. It wasn't that he was performed poorly at sports or that he hated them. The issue was that the parents felt entitled and expected their kid to want to bond over sports too. They wanted him to love sports like they did. They had a view of how their family and kids would be, dating back from when they were dating. They just assumed that each kid would be a mini-me, with muscle and bike shorts, but they weren't.

The pressure their teen felt to conform, to fit in, and to gain their approval was at odds with his desire to develop himself and to create his own identity. He felt that he'd be disappointing his parents if he didn't play competitive sports in high school. He wouldn't be able to get the scholarships they wanted him to get; they wouldn't be able to go to his games; get ice cream afterward; post his stats, team pics, and videos; and so on. It would really be a big loss and a hit to the family's assumed and chosen culture and norms.

Now, it would have been easy for the parents to save face with their friend group, which they'd formed (and had grown to love) when their kids started participating in sports together, by saying that they just want their teen to be happy and do what he wanted, even though they felt very sad and disappointed that they probably would be judged or somehow left out of the friend group.

It would also have been easy for them to assume that athletes are better-quality friends than musicians or artists; that he wouldn't possibly get college paid for or help the family with college expenses if he quit sports; or that he would become unhealthy and out of shape if he didn't go to practice and participate in the athletic culture. It would have been easy for them also to try to convince him to stick to sports by reminding him of his accomplishments and improvements, the fun trips he'd taken, or the friends he'd made. They could say that it was just a phase. They could say that he'd thank them later for making him stick it out. They could go on and on about the negatives of quitting and that it would ruin his self-image. They could blame others for their bad influence on him or call him lazy or unmotivated. You can see how they could take multiple approaches to making him remain an athlete.

It also would be much easier for the boy to "suck it up" and just take the path of least resistance; to not enact courage; to not have the freedom, safety, and security (even if only in his mind) to say to them that what they wanted for him was not aligned with the person he was becoming, which he knew was really him, deep in his heart. Even though he didn't value his participation as they did, though he pretended to do so for quite some time, he was missing an opportunity to develop himself in a new way that he truly desired.

I'm not saying that all the ideas parents have about what quitting means aren't valid; many of them are. What I am saying, though, is that we, as parents, create a lot of assumptions and expectations, maybe from when we were teenagers, dreaming of our own much-better family than the one we got stuck with or a family that mirrored our own family. Parents may infuse unquestioned beliefs and practices into their homes that are out of love and care for their precious children, but these can be the underlying cause of strife and disconnection and pain between parents and teens.

We don't mean to be entitled or to want compliance and results that are born of our own needs, visions, and dreams. When the other half of the equation is not considered, the child, who is actually a developing human of their own design, there will be conflict. When our children only align with but a few of our own personal needs/

vision/dreams, we don't want to be disappointed, but it's natural. We aren't mean, but it's also not necessarily how we'd like to be treated either, right?

I mean how many stories do we have to watch on movies, read in books and hear from friends and relive from our own lives, of people feeling they aren't free to be who they are, do what they love, pursue their own dreams because they feel obligated to please someone else, a mother or a father? There often is pressure to be something, to prove something, to be successful, not even realizing that success is not one thing, one profession, or one lifestyle; it's not *one* anything at all.

Look hard. Are you entitled? Are your expectations cemented in your mind, in your heart? Do you feel a need to measure up to someone else's expectations? Are you doing it not only in your own life but in your child's as well? You have to face this. You have to ask yourself: What am I gaining, and what is there to lose in assuming that my teenagers are as similar to me as they pretend to be, in order to gain or maintain my approval?

Do as I Say, Not as I Do

I'll never forget witnessing the dad who smacked the back of his son's head while yelling, "Don't hit your sister!"

As ironic and sad as that is, consider that we, as parents, do the same sort of thing sometimes, even though it does seem mean and messed up, and it does make us entitled.

See if any of these descriptions fit for you:

- We are rude (and justify it) but tell our kids to not speak in the same condescending, rude, or sarcastic tone.
- We are head-down in our phones/computers (and justify it), but we tell our teens they are too obsessed with their screens.
- We don't care very well for our physical environment (but have great reasons why), but we constantly tell our kids to clean their own spaces.

- We drop our phones or lose something important but then have no mercy on our kids for their own accidents.
- We drink heavily (because we are of age) but preach against the kids' alcohol consumption.

All of these are versions of our feeling entitled to get different results—and better ones—from our teens, while we feel fine in our covert and overt practices, which actually defy the sermons we preach.

This is tough. What would you have to give up or clean up to have more influence on your teenager? I don't mean the fear-based influence—the kind that comes from power—or the I'm-the-boss mentality. I mean genuine influence.

It's common for teenagers to justify and rationalize their own dangerous or unkind behavior when they see it, hear it, or feel it in their own homes. If you want respect, you must earn it. (Eeek! I said it.) Don't we say that to our kids? The same is true of trust. "You have to earn my trust," we may say, or "Earn it back," yet we don't follow the same basic rules of life, and our kids know it.

The most difficult thing about dealing with teenagers is not that they *think* they are right as much as that they *are* right. It can be very confronting. They have a much purer view of what is right and wrong and what makes sense and what doesn't. The humility it takes to admit when your teenagers are right and that they uncovered hypocrisy in you or that you hid behind your title could fill an ocean.

In other words, they haven't sold out yet and become callous, numb, and/or accepting that people are not what they say they are. They are angry about it! They can't believe it when they find out that the rules and regulations that they've been told to observe are just for them and not for everyone, not even you. They can't stomach that fact that their parents lied to them or misled them or manipulated them. They can't believe that they can be spoken to like they are worthless; that they can be blamed and put down in the name of "I love you, and that's why I have to say this or do this," yet they are punished and corrected for treating their parents or siblings in the same hurtful ways.

Symptoms

You may have been tempted to call on examples and evidence of your teenager's personal brand of entitlement as you read this section. Let's look at what they believe they should get in return for little or nothing: good grades, privileges, nice things, fitness, money, trust, playing in a game versus sitting on the bench, being included socially. Look closely (and it helps to do this objectively, like a science experiment, so it doesn't feel personal to you), and see if you can make some connections to the mindset that has them operating in ways that don't work and that leave you feeling frustrated with the way you do life.

Another good place to look for your influence on your child, occurring as entitlement, is in your parenting style. Do you despise entitlement in theory but are too soft on having your teenagers suffer in the good ways that will leave them feeling accomplished and that they earned something? Do you take the easy way, letting them take the easy way out and perpetuating their entitlement?

Future Implications of Being Entitled

If we go down a path of being righteous and unable to see our own faults, and we expect our kids to be like us or like someone else— someone they are not—we likely will pay a price in the next ten years. If we continue to act as if our own way of operating—our own entitlement to do whatever we want while insisting that our teens do things in a different way—is okay, we are not likely to have the future relationship and the access we would like to have in our teenagers' lives.

We might look back and wish that we had gotten more comfortable with coming down a few notches in our expectations and that we had related to the kid in front of us, not the one we wanted to see. We don't want to stand in the future and sadly mourn the loss of our child's connection with us because we were caught up in appearances, affiliations, and approval.

You can change things, starting now, by answering this question: How am I acting in an entitled way in my role as parent, in my relationship with my teen? Your toughness and hard line on how to live life may not get you the result you thought it would.

Authoritarian

The Old School Is Out

In previous generations, it was probably just called *parenting*. The outcomes and behaviors are similar to being entitled, but the authoritarian philosophy is more counter to having a fully functioning relationship than you may realize.

When we are drill sergeants—Miss Hannigan–style (from *Annie*), my-way-or-the-highway type of parents—we miss out on opportunities to teach our kids to compromise and to consider other people's needs, preferences, goals, timelines, and feelings. We set them up to seek other more controlling, authoritative types in their friend groups or romantic interests. They are less likely to question authority, even when the authority does *not* have their best interests at heart, as you do.

You may be authoritarian to keep things simple and to enjoy the hierarchical set up that only benefits the top tier. You might operate this way; if you want willing and eager cooperation, however, I will show you how to have the cooperation without the control piece. We don't want to create yes-people who do what they're told. We do want to raise people who are confident and thoughtful when no one is telling them when to jump while also learning to be respectful and responsible at the same time.

Gotta Look the Part

A vacation, a family reunion, or a holiday photo session comes up, and after we've paid too little attention to what is going on with our teens, we still expect or feel entitled to have this high-stakes event go well, to show others and to prove to ourselves that there is peace and harmony in the family, when really, there is not.

Teens often tell me that they feel like all their parents care about is that their family looks perfect from the outside; that they are to jump through the hoops just right and play the part in front of others. Their parents act like the kids are so sweet, kind, and cool when thirty seconds earlier, they threatened or insulted them out of fear that the kids would mess up.

The type of resentment and push-back that this sort of pressure and falseness creates is severe. If parents could see that, they would be more likely to gain the enthusiasm and cooperation for which they are desperate; if they paid as close attention to the details of their teens lives as they do to which pops of color they're going to wear in the family pictures, they would be surprised.

We cannot jump from high point to high point in our lives and expect everyone to appreciate the view if we don't tend to the pain that comes from navigating the valleys. There will be bigger and nastier blowups in times of stress when real issues have been ignored and parents have been controlling, have failed to listen, or haven't respected or considered what their child needs.

Punishment Is a No-No

According to Michael Eric Dyson, a professor of sociology at Georgetown University, "The point of discipline is to transmit values to children. The purpose of punishment is to coerce compliance and secure control, and failing that, to inflict pain as a form of revenge."[1]

---

[1] Michael Eric Dyson, "Punishment or Child Abuse," *New York Times*, September 17, 2014, https://www.nytimes.com/2014/09/18/opinion/punishment-or-child-abuse.html.

When our main goal is compliance to the behavior that makes us feel comfortable and in control, we miss the entire point of parenting, which is to teach and guide our children so they can become adults who think critically and make the best choices.

Here's something I say to my clients without fail: You must stop yanking your kids' Xbox, computer, phone, and keys as punishment when the reason you are doing it is to show them who's boss. It's a cheap power play. It ends discussion. It thwarts learning. It enrages the kids, and now, all energy and thought goes into the fact that you've taken away something that matters to them.

How can we expect teens to think about what they've done when they are reeling from the fact that we just took away their lifeline to their friends, the most important aspect of their existence? I'm referring to when the thing that's taken away is not related to the issue, when it's more like a trigger response to the parent's being mad or feeling out of control.

There's no teaching. There's no trust built. In fact, we just make our kids into smarter bad guys who learn how to avoid getting in trouble. They can expertly learn to play the game of not getting punished, but that does not mean that they aren't still doing the things that lead them to a path of real trouble. Now, however, they are sneakier. They don't believe that you'll ever rationally respond to a problem or mistake they make, so your access to them gets smaller. The thing you want to avoid—their getting in too deep with any of life's perils but not coming to you for help—is basically guaranteed to happen.

Time to Skill Up

If we jump to conclusions, triggered by a behavior, a tone, a grade, or a show of irresponsibility, then we make the next jump to exerting our power and making our teenagers suffer, hoping it will scare them into submission, it's a sign that we need to level up our parenting game. In other words, it's time to increase our skills so we can do better.

Perhaps no one modeled for you how to sit down and talk. Perhaps no one who parented you was capable of reacting to something that was "wrong" or "bad" without using anger. It's time to learn some more tricks.

Not only do our kids mirror the same anger that we spew out, but they quickly will learn how to punish us in return. It's a cycle that breeds hate and division. It's incredibly short-sighted. It builds up like snow on a steep mountainside; then, one day, it ends up crushing both of you like an avalanche.

Punishment is the equivalent of bullying in many cases. It's like having a beef with someone on the playground. Rather than talking it out to find common ground, seek understanding, and make a plan for going forward, the bully just punches the other kids in the face and walks away. The same issues are still present. The source of the issue isn't uncovered. The root of the misunderstanding or any possibility for authentic improvement is overlooked, and all that's left is one person who exerted strength and another lying on the ground with a bloody nose.

Why is talking with and trying to relate to our teens harder than a snap judgment and a punitive solution? It may be because parents are so often led to believe—likely by their own parents—that using the inherent power dynamic between parents and kids is the only way to parent.

Our kids know we aren't perfect. Our kids know we are human. When we pretend that we aren't and place ourselves at the top of the food chain—like an irritable lion that is ready to pounce and rip apart the gazelles—we are not fooling them. We are creating more of us, more power-hungry lions that want to rip someone else apart—and likely, we are first on the list.

You Will Pay for That

My teenage clients have told me dozens of stories of the lengths to which they go to make their parents pay for their authoritarian stunts. I'll share a few with you.

A fourteen-year-old boy pretended to be a political Conservative in a home of Liberals, just to upset his parents. He didn't believe any bit of what he pretended to stand for, but he enjoyed that his parents were upset and offended by his rhetoric. It was the one way he could hold on to some dignity, a little power, and a shred of self-respect. He decided to sell out (even if just publicly) on his own morals to upset his parents by putting on a red hat, which infuriated them. Infuriating them was the whole point.

A girl of eleven told me that just as she was gearing up to clean her room—she had a plan for organizing and creating some order, something she authentically wanted in her space—her mom came in and yelled at her for her room being messy. The girl chose to abort her mission because she did not want to give her mom the satisfaction of getting what she wanted. She would rather suffer in her "disgusting" room than please her mom. Her mom had not given her the space and time to come to her own conclusion of wanting a clean room. There are a lot of messy rooms out there that exist solely to torture parents.

A fifteen-year-old nonbinary kid (nonbinary means that they don't identify as exclusively male or female and sometimes use the pronouns they/them/theirs instead of he/him/his or she/her/hers) told me that they don't want to give in to the extreme pressure that their parents put on them to take honors classes and pull all A's. They are fully capable of the work and the thinking and truly want the results, but they would rather have their parents be upset with them because they don't want to be pressured and controlled into meeting their parents' expectations.

Get this: the kid *wanted what the parents wanted*, sincerely, but because of how tough the parents were on them about it, they chose to resist in order to maintain their dignity, rather than comply with their parents' desires. They purposely and systematically achieved below their actual capability.

A fourteen-year-old boy told his mom he wanted to learn guitar. His mom got extremely excited; she got him a teacher, a guitar, and books; she made him practice and sent him videos. She imposed her excitement on him in such an overbearing (if well-meaning) way that he felt pressured and controlled by her, and so he told her that he was quitting. Fast-forward a year: we were having a session in his playroom, and he pulled out a guitar from its case, which had been stashed out of the way, and started playing it skillfully.

"I didn't know you played," I told him. "That sounded great."

He looked up at me with fear in his eyes. "Please don't tell my mom!"

Confused, I said, "Okay. Why not?"

This was when he told me how she had gotten "obsessed" with this idea and took away his feeling of fun and curiosity for it, so he secretly had learned to play using YouTube. He didn't want her to have the satisfaction of knowing he had met his goal.

Do you see? The power thing has a hidden dark side. You think you're up against a kid who is lazy, who loves to live like a pig, who hates order, who doesn't care if they "waste" their potential, but really, they are posturing so that you don't get to win every single time. The self-respect they crave and the autonomy and self-sufficiency they are trying to develop is more important to them than pleasing their parents. They'd rather suffer their parents being disappointed, even if it means selling out on themselves.

It's Not Too Late to Say Sorry

A major theme of authoritarian parenting is the inability to stand down and admit when we have made a mistake, jumped to conclusions, reacted to harshly, or made a rash decision. "That's the way it is" is the law of the land. Resentment, even hatred, grows in the teen's heart. Regret grows in the parent's heart. It's hard to come back from that bossy, dictator style and to admit you're learning as you go, but the exponential impact of continuing to posture like you're all-knowing, almighty, and without flaws is the stuff of destroyed relationships.

Humility and vulnerability are the bravest route. We don't lose face or respect when we admit, readily and often, that we are in over our heads. It's okay to say to our kids that we don't know how to handle this, that we want to take time to feel it out before making a decision, and that we want to gain our teen's input and proceed together, one step at a time. It's amazing how we will get the cooperation and respect we think we deserve if we come down off the parenting throne and be with the people.

The pressure to know how to handle everything masterfully and do it right may leave us feeling, ironically, like we don't know how to succeed. If so, it's time to reduce the pressure and give ourselves permission to be human. It's time to admit when we are inconsistent, fear-based, misusing our power, and not giving our teens an opportunity to contribute to their own growth. It's time to foster teamwork in the relationship.

Future Implications of Authoritarian Parenting

As soon as they can go, they are gone. As soon as they can escape the oppression that they experience, they will be with someone who listens, who cares about their thoughts; they choose them. On the other hand, they may be comfortable operating inside the cycle called "be human, get punished, comply, avoid punishment, repeat" that they seek that out in others and end up being controlled and under the spell of someone who doesn't have their best interests at heart, but instead appreciates their compliant nature because it serves their own needs.

Whether they defy you and reject you as the authority you've created yourself to be or they replace you with someone who wants to take advantage of their trained spinelessness, you will not have the chance to genuinely know your kid or to contribute to them in the way you'd like.

Numb

Conforming Equals Numbness, and
Numbness Equals Conforming

I am convinced that, in most cases, if we were curious about what our teenagers think and why, we would remember that we too once held similar, beautifully idealistic, stubborn, and unrelenting views. As life went on, however, we gave in to the pressure to conform, to reduce conflict, to play safe, and to follow along with what was expected and required of us. We really didn't love it and weren't as proud of it as we may have pretended we were.

The irony is that having kids is a big part of why we grow up and have to face reality, and then we need to let go of our dreams and the things that once really lit us up. It happens slowly, but I'm here to say to you, with all the love in my heart, that we need you back. We (yes, I speak on behalf of humanity from time to time) need you to remember and take steps toward getting back to that teenager you were—the one who believed in something that was pure, who loved something so much, and who would fight to the death if anyone tried to convince you not to go for it.

If you don't relate to being that way as a teen, consider that you might have been somewhat oppressed. That dull ache or dissatisfaction you may feel from time to time—or every time you wake up—could be because you never got to fully express yourself because your parents were entitled to having their kids be the way they expected.

(Siri, find a therapist near me.) I know this might be hard to look at, and maybe this is not the right time, or the ideas I'm sharing don't fit you. You don't have to buy what I'm pitching. I'm just showing where you can look to help meet your goal: to be closer to your teen. You want a relationship that really works.

When Tapping Out Seems Like the Best Alternative

Checked out; mind foggy. This type of "mean" usually isn't of the aggressive flavor. It's more along the lines of dropping the ball—not being on the inside of what is happening with our teens. We often just feel sort of dead inside, like we can't take *one more thing*. We pour a glass of wine, take a puff of whatever, and press "next episode" one more time. We become less attentive and less able to be there to notice what is going on with our teens or to read their behaviors and moods with accuracy.

In fact, our kids may appear numb too—everyone in their own space, with their own numbing tools, just coming out to eat and maybe say *hey* on their way to the kitchen.

It's too hard to deal with life. Quiet and separate are easier. Being alone or out socializing is easier. Staying at work is easier. Getting buzzed is easier.

Numbness Masquerading as Judgment

I worked with a family in which the father would come home from work in the evenings while the homework, moods, fatigue and patience levels of the wife and kids were all at their max capacity. He'd go straight to his room for the rest of the night, having gotten dinner on the way home so that he could avoid the messiness of homework time, which "should have been done by now." He was avoiding the chaos of the strewn sports and music equipment, backpacks, and books, which "should have been hung on the hooks and put in the cubbies right away." He sharply criticized his wife—in front of their four daughters—for "doing a terrible job running the home" and "for not setting a good example of a leader" for their four daughters,

He could not handle the reality of his own home—the discomfort of things not being perfect, ideal, under control, and "right" so that he could relax—so he went to his room and escaped the family, blaming them for his retreat. He left early for work in the morning to avoid the stress of the morning routine too. The impact on his wife and girls was immense.

His legacy: If you're stressed out, just check out, and make sure you blame everyone as being wrong on your way to your room.

I Can't Even

It's understandable that when you reach the point where you cannot handle one more stressor, unmet expectation, mistake, or challenge, you'd want to find a way to calm down and feel less of all of that. The ability to cope with what raising teenagers and being a human being at the same time brings, day after day, is imperative! We must be able to cope.

Now, the question at hand is, how do you cope? Were you taught how to cope? Do you regret your actions, reactions, tone, and words when you reach your maximum capacity of stress? That's a sign that you may need to improve your coping skills. We do tell this to our kids, but do we practice it ourselves?

There's a temptation to justify our less-than-optimal behavior because no one else knows what it's like to be us or how hard it is—that's something parents can hang their hats on 'til the end of time. It's one option for sure. Someday, we think, when the kids have mortgages, businesses, bills, marriages, and their own kids, they will feel the same awful, stressed-out way that we do, and then they'll say, "I get why Mom always had a wine glass in her hand," or "I get why Dad hid out in the bathroom for an hour at a time, pretending to go poop."

Let's look at another option. What if the numbing out and the freaking out that normally precedes the numbing could be avoided to a great extent because there was a sense of calm? What if, in your family, the people took a deep breath, took time to focus on one thing at a time, and prioritized people over schedules and feelings over metrics, like grades and performance? What if, in your family, the people were highly productive and focused, and there was a sense of grace and mercy too? No one felt the need to push themselves or each other to the absolute limits of emotional, physical, and mental bankruptcy.

We know this: drugs, alcohol, avoidance, rage, checking out, getting sucked in, overindulging, and perfectionism are ways to numb ourselves. And we numb ourselves because we don't invest the time or effort to learn a healthy way to cope with the inevitable stress of having teenagers, a family, and all of its trappings without feeling trapped.

Vicarious Living

One pitfall I see often is when parents are numb to their own needs, self-care, goals, and dreams while being like a walking nerve ending about their teenagers' lives. I have seen mothers and fathers who are obsessed with the following areas—sometimes one parent obsesses over all of the following; sometimes the areas are divided among two or four parents (including stepparents); sometimes each parent puts all their might into attempting to control these areas:

> *Grades*: I've worked with parents who say their teenager's A- test score wasn't up to par, when the class average was a C+. I've seen parents punish their teenagers for not getting straight A's, when one-tenth of a percentage was the difference between an A and a B. Kids have told me that their parents text them moment to moment, based on the teachers' input in the gradebook apps, saying, "Why did you miss 2/10 on your science quiz today?"—even before the kid knew it was graded. They text their kids throughout the day about their disappointments. Some parents have tutors for their

kids during off-school hours, pushing their kids to their farthest limits. These parents think that will make the difference, but they are simply exhausting their kids in every way and not listening to the kids' overt and covert messages of "I can't go on like this!" I know kids who go home the long way because they know their parents will greet them at the door with their lists of homework, failures, and ways to improve their academic standings.

Effort: Even when grades are good (which I do not believe is the ultimate indicator of health, success or happiness), parents will critique the amount of perceived effort a child applies to a variety of tasks, from school to chores. They'll say, "Their room is clean, but it's not as clean as it would be if I'd done it. They don't put their heart into it." Parents will say, "I know they did okay, but they are smart. They spoke when they were ten months old. Their first-grade teacher said they were the brightest kid they'd ever met, so they must be lazy because they got 87 percent on their honors bio quiz instead of 100 percent"

Appearance: Well-meaning parents want to protect their kids from being judged or looked down upon in this cruel world, so they will choose a topic like clothes, hair, makeup, weight, or posture and hold on tight. Parents will try to convince their teen to change something about how they present themselves through mandates, passive-aggressive comments, direct criticism, manipulation, and/ or teasing. Parents will lock on to something that bothers them about how their teens express themselves and will not let up. This turns something that either doesn't need to be handled or could easily be handled with respect and teaching into a constant and frustrating theme in the relationship, causing a divide and a distraction from having a meaningful conversation or relationship.

Future: In many different cultures and demographics, parents will often become extremely focused on how their kid's life will look on a college application, job application and even to impress future in-laws. A strong focus on volunteer work, joining clubs and organizations, elite sports teams, honors classes, academic summer camps, test-prep courses, language immersion, are all good things and total blessings for the kids in many ways, but there is a downside as well. I'm not knocking the idea of giving our kids opportunities and setting them up for a great future with a variety of options. I'm saying that the parental pursuit of success can sometimes go awry when kids are pushed, when they fear they won't measure up, and when a trend toward more, more, more can seem like pressure to the teen. Many teens, from as young as thirteen, have told me that they feel like they are a project to their parents. The kids can see clearly that their parents are consumed with turning out an impressive "product" and making sure their own parents and social circles see that they are good parents because of their kids' achievements, scores, talents, rankings, and abilities. Kids often believe that their parents don't care about or enjoy them unless they measure up to their parents' expectations.

Sports/Music/Performance-Based Activities: If you're holding on tightly to your teenager's becoming a phenom in any given talent or practiced-based endeavor—sports, games, music, contests, pageants, social media following, etc.—you may want to check in with yourself. Is this about you or is this about them? Have you given them a choice? Are they happy? This relates to producing impressive "products." You likely know if you're doing this, but it takes courage to start this conversation and possibly get untangled from the activity.

Gender/Sexuality: If we have a problem with who our children are, and if we have firm, not-based-on-reality expectations that they will show up "normally" in their gender expression and identification and to whom they are attracted and love, that means we are numb—maybe even dead—to something that we need to revive—stat!

Having a child, whether born to us biologically, adopted, inherited, or otherwise, is not picking a snack from a vending machine. ("Hm-m-m. I choose ... A-7." *Kerplunk*.) It's like putting our hands into a mystery grab bag while wearing a blindfold and thick gloves and not finding out what we get until possibly several years later, if we're lucky.

If we think that it's our job to decide for and tell another person if they are acceptable (in general and specifically to us, as parents), then we are not in touch with the primary role we have as parents—as protectors and nurturers of another soul. We are to love them, no matter what—*literally, no matter what.* We don't get to bail out and call them sinners or blame our rejection (no matter how subtle or overt) on God or whatever. We must love them full-out, nonstop, to the point that we are their single biggest champion and hero—that is, if and when we get so lucky that they let us know more about the unfolding mystery of who they are.

To assume things such as that your child will identify with the biological gender (male or female) as soon as the reveal-party cake is cut to shows blue or pink is not a safe bet. To assume that your child will be straight because you are straight and you're comfortable with straight people and so is your family or your church or your God or your culture is also not a safe bet. To assume that your child will be a male, identify with that body, and then proceed to express himself with "boy" clothes, "boy" activities, "boy" mannerisms and pronouns and be attracted to girls is not a safe bet. To assume that your biologically female child will identify with her body and then proceed to express herself with "girl" clothes, "girl" activities, "girl" mannerisms and pronouns, and be attracted to boys is not a safe bet.

The only thing that is our right to bet on is how much we will be able to love and accept our children just as they are and just as they tell us they are. We must not reduce our love, acceptance, interest, comfort level, pride, and joy in who our children are because they don't fit into our expectations, which came from thin air.

Personality: Your teenager may not laugh at what you laugh at and may not cry at what makes you cry. They may hate what you love. They may love what drives you crazy. They might be weird or cool, while you may be the opposite. They may be sociable or quiet, while you may be the opposite. We must not numb ourselves by worrying or obsessing over what our kids ought to like and be like. We must instead become acutely sensitive to what they do like and what they are like. Personalities are not to be resisted; they are to be appreciated. If we "can't stand" something about our teenager's personality, that says more about us and our capacity for acceptance, wisdom, and grace than it does about how our teens are.

The above gives you a flavor of the types of issues that parents can be hyper-focused on and use as a way to avoid handling their own lives. We could make a full-time job out of any aspect of our teens and what they could and should be doing better. It's nice that we care, and yes, they should be thankful they aren't being ignored or neglected, but there's a point at which this type of hyper-focus becomes an excuse for parents to not handle their own lives.

It's easy to see something in someone else, but it's harder to examine our own focus and priorities. We must see if, for any reason, we are more concerned with how our kids are operating, looking, and feeling than we are with ourselves and our other important relationships. Otherwise, we are missing a vital component of parenting, which is to model personal responsibility.

Being numb on one front while being extra vigilant on another—avoiding our own lives while being an FBI agent about theirs; neglecting ourselves on multiple levels and putting all that time and energy into another person—is dangerous. I want to tell you that you can be a good, aware, engaged parent and still take a few steps back. It may sting, but you need to admit that your anxiety is creating a numbness that leads to self-neglect and points you away from dealing with your own growth opportunities.

Future Implications of Being Numb

If we operate in a haze and a state of distraction, escape, and avoidance—as parents and as people in general—we likely yearn for the peace, satisfaction, and contentment that comes from being grounded when we do the hard work to heal our wounds and seek mental, emotional, and physical health.

The various tools of distraction and escape that we use to avoid ourselves can ruin our lives. Addiction, seeking control, being out of control, and not having a solid foundation of freedom and choice are all dangerous and, sadly, widely suffered (and, therefore, accepted) ways to operate. It takes our being vulnerable and having the courage to step out of the fog of distraction and addiction to start on a path of clarity.

Sometimes, it's a slow trend that starts small, and it can be shocking to find yourself in a place of unhealthy thinking or operating. It may cover your pain or impede your judgment and ability to express your deep love for your teenager, and that's when you know it's time to face it head-on.

MEAN Summary

Please understand that I do *not* think you're mean or intend pain or injury. If you've used any of the components of the MEAN acronym to judge yourself or to be ashamed or disappointed in yourself, I want you to please stop. Please.

If you're feeling angry, annoyed, or defensive because you saw yourself in the MEAN acronym, I want you to understand two things: I am not judging you, and you don't need to judge yourself either. The urge to judge is so automatic that you may not see it right away, but it's a big part of what makes parenting your teen hard and is definitely at the root of why your own life feels hard.

When this type of judgment occurs inside us, we want to believe we can hold it in, but it oozes out of us—we don't have a choice. When our confidence and self-esteem are all in the toilet, we grasp at straws.

The *mi*sunderstandings, *e*ntitlement, *a*uthoritarian power grabs, and *n*umbed escape mode are all a function of how *mean* we are to ourselves as we try to navigate the hardest job in the universe: parenting.

When our kids get to the homestretch of childhood and look forward to their own adulthood, they will notice and react to our adult style. They stop being our audience and hop up on the stage to question our direction, methods, and intentions. While this may look like a nightmare at first glance, consider that iron sharpens iron. Raising a teenager could be the very thing that has you level up in your life.

We don't intend to be mean to our kids; we just get reactive— that's probably more accurate. There's only so much input and decision-making one person can take. You are facing your greatest challenge. It's not just you versus this crazy world, or you versus human nature (yours and your teen's), but it's also you versus you.

Anyone who has had a child in their care and feels a deep sense of responsibility—even pressure—to succeed in tending to the child's physical, emotional, mental and spiritual health; safety; education; social life; present, future, and the way they remember their past; and how they see themselves, as well as ensuring that they'll function in society and be able to do the dishes and their own laundry, knows there isn't a more complex and difficult task in the history of the world.

The short-term effects of being misunderstood, entitled, authoritarian, and/or numb are that we miss out on the little moments and the big opportunities to be on the inside of our teens' lives. We are not considered an ally. They won't turn to us first when life gets real; in fact, we may be last.

The long-term effect of being misunderstood, entitled, authoritarian, and/or numb is that we model that way of operating, and our teens may be the same way with us and with their siblings, peers, future mates, and colleagues. It's funny how the very thing we often don't like in certain fundamental relationships are the very things we tend to repeat or seek.

You don't want your teen to show up, with you and in life, as misunderstood and unable to ask for help; unable to communicate feelings and needs; feeling entitled and wanting a higher quality of things than what they have earned or created; acting like an authoritarian; demanding that the world work in their favor because of their title or role; and/or numb and checked out of reality, so we, as parents, need to keep going!

Before we proceed, please take a moment to say the following statement aloud or whisper it, write it down on the inside cover of this book, or text it to yourself. Let it sink in. (Perhaps an interpretive dance would be nice!)

I promise to be kind, open-minded, and gentle with myself and for myself. I will seek to use my beginner's mind to explore a new way of creating a fully functioning relationship with my teen.

Part 2
REAL

Let go of who you think you're supposed
to be; embrace who you are.
—Brené Brown

Being REAL is really at the root of operating in a clean and functional way with our teenagers. There's nothing a teenager can sniff out faster than someone who is hiding behind a facade, playing the part, and posing or pretending to be something they are not.

I wonder if they hate that so much because they feel that urge to be false themselves as they try to create their own identities through different phases and styles of expressing themselves. They want to know who they are and to be authentic, regardless of how lost or caught up they may seem sometimes.

There are infinite advantages to finding out where we are being inauthentic and how that inadvertent choice impacts so many areas of our lives. It takes a certain strength of heart to put yourself under a microscope and see that who you're being in your life is misaligned who you really are. I believe you can do this. Remember that this an *anything* in the statement we hold deep in our beings as parents: I will do *anything* for my child.

The Role

We adopt a certain role when we leave the hospital or the place where we first are introduced to our children. It's time to turn up the pressure cooker! *You are a parent now!* Those words must weigh one hundred times more than the average everyday word. We are complete rookies, in most cases, yet we have 100 percent responsibility from day one. There's no internship to learn the ropes. It's like—*boom!*—you're the CEO on your first day of work. *Pressure.*

It's normal to inadvertently create a facade of confidence and even defensiveness when we are new at something, and the various on-lookers have so much advice, experience, and wisdom that we don't have yet. It's natural to want to be the best for our babies or to already be good at it. It's a terrifying thought to realize that our growing-up process will be in tandem with our children's in many ways.

As a mom of five kids, who were five years old and younger at one point, I gave myself *no* space, not one quarter inch, to admit that I was having a hard time with my mental health, my self-care, or my kids. I felt like, "Hey, I got myself into this mess, so why should I whine about it?" The facade was hardening. I looked great, as much as possible. I acted like I knew what the hell I was doing. I pressed myself to be one who was perceived in a way that others would think—and, I hoped, even say—"Wow! She has it together."

Vulnerability was not an option for me. Not everyone handles it like that, though.

Leggo My Ego

You might not like to think of it this way, but try it on for a second and see if this gives you a new perspective. This might sting for a beat, but it also might give you an opening for some new freedom. Here it is:

Do you think you have an ego? We all do, but that is the most common block that parents have in parenting in a way that gets the short- and long-term results they want. Specifically, when parents lead with their egos, there is very little change or improvement possible for the teen and the parent.

Let's check in with these signs that your ego is running the show:

Do you compare yourself to others; specifically, to their "perfect" kids, marriages, lives, bodies, or vacations? Or you are the "perfect" one who feels superior to others, even if it's a deep-down thing, and you act very down-to-earth and real on the surface?

Do you misread situations or people and then want to blame yourself or someone else?

When things don't go your way or the "right" way, do you immediately find fault in others?

Do you set impossible goals that don't account for humanity and the impossibility of controlling external factors? Then, when you don't reach those goals, do you get down on yourself?

Do you spend time talking and thinking about others' flaws—or your own?

Do you find it hard to back down in an argument? Do you need to be right, win, or have the last word?

All of these are human ways of thinking, particularly in teens, but you, as an adult, with the advantage of a fully formed frontal lobe—this part of the brain is not fully developed until age twenty-five—are officially in charge. I challenge you to check your own tendencies to do all of the above. Being "REAL" will give you new options that will allow you to have the freedom to be more effective and peaceful.

Hands in the Air; I Surrender

Another version of a facade is to pretend that we are being overrun by kids, life, and everything else and that "that's the way it is," and we don't have a choice. We say, "Let's just buckle up for eighteen-plus years of chaos and hope for the best." This way of operating is not authentic because it's a way out of the learning, growing, and changing that are required to adapt to the challenges that parenting poses.

Some parents are not at either of these extremes of ego or total surrender, but many are. When we think we are obligated to talk, behave, and respond in a certain way to save face and to look like we are okay with what is happening, we limit our options and, therefore, become less free and able to be ourselves. We let our egos and our need for approval run the show, instead of our intuition, gut, or higher self getting the last word.

Parental Blackout

One notable phenomenon is that parents seem to black out when it comes to remembering what it was like when they were teenagers. They take a moral high ground about right and wrong and forget that part of growing up is messing up and falling flat on their faces.

Think about a time when you failed at something. You might have shared that failure with someone, but it was hard to muster the courage to do that. Then that person went on about how wrong and dumb it was of you and tells you all the ways you could have done better.

Now, think of a time when you failed and shared it with someone, and the person to whom you opened up told you when they had a hard time like that too, maybe even worse. They tell you that they were okay, and you'll be okay too.

Is there a rule book somewhere that says we have to be so proper and stuffy? Parents often believe that their kids will use that anything they share with them against them, so they are very private about their own lives, but I am on the side of being real—within reason. Still, that's how we teach; we must first meet our teens where we are, not where they should be.

Let's break down the acronym REAL:

> Resilient
> Effective
> Authentic
> Loving

Resilient

Goal: Resilient Kids

We want to raise resilient kids. We want them to be able to withstand the pressures and inevitable failures that life will bring, to grow, to learn, and to not be reduced to a puddle of snot every time something doesn't work out the way they wanted.

Goal: Resilient Parents

I'm about to turn resilience back on us as parents. When our kids flop around life, not "getting it," and we are in the wrong place at the wrong time—in the middle of a hairy, greasy, teenage emotional breakdown—we get a little spittle on our faces, a snarky or angry word thrown our way, or a door slammed in our faces. Do we get angry and make it all about us and respect? Do we say that if we had talked that way to our parents, we would have gotten knocked into next week?

Or do we take a step back and decide to hold off 'til things cool off before talking about the dangers of violent door-slamming and then think about what must be going on inside their heads and hearts that would have them in so much pain? Do we think about how we could best support them, or do we freak out and make it worse?

This is what I think about when I talk to parents about resiliency. Can you train yourself and intentionally practice not making it about you when they even say they are mad at you? People in pain often resort to scapegoating and blame. People can go on and on about one issue, only to realize later that it was about something else completely. People sometimes have emotional responses to subjects before they can think rationally.

People get triggered. Teens do, and so do parents.

Resiliency is about modeling how stable you can be under pressure. Can you hug your teens while they are crying, or do you tell them to suck it up? Can you bear their illogical rants, knowing that they just need to pour it all out?

What Else?

My favorite question to ask my own kids when they are upset is, "What else?" Here's an example:

Teen: Ugh! It's not fair that you won't let me go with my friends!

Parent: I know. What else are you mad about? [Don't disagree. Wait. Be quiet.]

Teen: I hate that my friends are going without me. I feel left out.

Parent: What else?

Teen: I think they don't really like me.

Parent: [Don't ask why, and don't disagree.] What else?

Teen: I messed up and said something rude to my friend because I was jealous.

Parent: What else?

Teen: I haven't been sleeping well.

Parent: [Don't tell them how you're going to solve that for them.] What else?

Teen: I don't know. I think that's it.

The result is an emptied-out, ready-to-breathe teen, one who's ready to calm down or wind down the suffering portion of the evening and begin recovery and possible problem-solving.

What if the parent had yelled back, "*Fair* is just a place where they sell cotton candy! You're such a brat! Now you can't go out tonight *or* tomorrow either! Give me your phone, *now*!"

That parent would have missed out on important and relevant

information, as well as widening the divide between parent and teenager.

Why So Jumpy?

Resiliency also means not getting set off by every stimulus that you sense. It means letting stuff go sometimes, in light of the big picture. It means not taking things personally. It doesn't mean you are a machine without feelings. It means you more often say things like this: "Ouch. That hurt. It reminded me of something in my past." Or "Sometimes I picture Grandma walking in here in the middle of our life, judging the living crap out of me, and telling me I'm failing. Sorry I made that about me and reacted with anger. I get that you're struggling and that you need my help, not my judgment and anger."

It's about mental toughness and being able to rebound from your own mistakes. Think about the MEAN acronym. It is very hard to create and nurture resiliency when there is misunderstanding, entitlement, an authoritarian mindset, and a general numbness happening.

Consider that you misunderstand your own reactions; you don't have compassion or see what affects you in the moment, so you judge it as something wrong. You operate like you are entitled to a perfect, clean record, you are infallible as a parent, and you have a high level of pressure to not screwing this up. You are harsh with yourself. You believe there is one way to do this job, and you better not fail at it. Finally, you think that just checking out or avoiding pain will put it off long enough to make it disappear. Nope. To. All.

Release the Pressure Valve

Rather than running yourself ragged to avoid the possible pains and disappointments that life can bring, work on building yourself up strong, from the inside out, so that when a storm inevitably blows your way, you will be able to withstand the elements. A lot of parenting energy tends to go toward prevention of the unpreventable: pain, suffering, sadness, disappointment, disapproval, failure, rejection, abandonment, loss.

What if you could do the obvious work toward controlling what is reasonably within your control to safeguard yourself and your teenager from those things through education and character-building? What if you also expended a great deal of energy to teach yourself and your teenager to be the kind of confident, strong, and wise people who can see the big picture and to create a strong growth mindset?

Being resilient is more powerful than avoiding the hard things in life. It's exactly those hard things, once faced and overcome, that become the evidence that we are strong, capable, and confident. Keeping our lives smaller and "safer" is not the answer to having a good life. Living boldly and being our real selves is what makes us feel alive.

Let's turn our focus from putting pressure on ourselves and our teens to have a perfect, pain-free life and, instead, apply our focus to developing ourselves and our teens into the most tenacious and unstoppable versions of ourselves that we can be—a much smarter investment of our precious time and energy.

Future Implications of Being Resilient

There seems to be no limit to what life can bring, whether or not we are parents. Doing the deep work to find out what we need to do to heal our tender spots, triggers, and wounds can be very scary. We try to deal with our day-to-day, moment-to-moment lives, and we barely keep up, so does it makes sense to make it harder by digging up old junk?

The best way I can describe it is like this: you keep riding on the trail when your mountain bike has a flat. Yes, you're still going forward, but it's ruining your bike and using too much of your energy. When we have the patience to stop and do the required work to repair the damage, the rest of the ride will be so much easier, especially the hills and the jumps.

I started back in therapy this year. I had gone to therapy years before, for depression and my eating disorder, but it was a very long time ago. It was my dad's death that had me justify going back to talk to someone, but honestly, he didn't come up that much, nor did my grief. Talking to my therapist and having her listen and say things I hadn't thought to myself was so powerful. I worked out a lot of my past as it compared to where I was in my current life. The *me* who had gone to therapy fifteen years earlier was not the *me* I had become, obviously, so it was like an entirely new experience. It freed me up greatly to be able to reconcile things that still affected me from my childhood and my previous marriage.

Resiliency is about our capacity to bounce back from difficulties. I believe that dealing with our issues head-on and not being ashamed of them is the most important factor in becoming confident and capable of navigating the difficulties presented when we're parenting teens. They see us doing the work. If you've ever wanted your teen to talk to someone, but you don't think it's for you, this could be your opportunity to lead the way.

Effective

What do *real* and *effective* have to do with each other? When people are *real*, they often are highly effective at what they intend to cause in any given situation. For fun, though, let's look at an opposite example: Your new consultant, boss, or job applicant waltzes in, and they are 100 percent full of shit, full of themselves, and cocky as hell. They tell you their plan, vision, and accolades ad nauseam. They trip over their ego. It hurts to watch them be so clueless about how unbelievably false and icky they come off. Do you hear them? Do you respond well? Are you interested in their ideas? Do you relate to them, even 10 percent?

What if that's how we show up for our teens? What if we have good ideas, smart advice, or tools that would be useful for them? We have what it takes to be effective, but we block our own efficacy by acting like asses? And by *asses*, I mean adopting the attitude of, "This is how I do it. Get used to it. Adapt to the only way I know how [or want to] parent."

Not My Type

Sometimes, parents will decide they don't really get along with their teens because they are so different, and the relationship suffers or is even destroyed as a result.

When one of my daughters was five years old, I decided that I was the wrong mom for her. I was not effective. I didn't get her. She was way out on another planet, and I was not interested in figuring out how to adjust to be really honest. Her brother, eighteen months older, was like my mirror image: a linear thinker; a simple, very tame type of spirit who really cared about my approval; someone who loved rules, plans, and structure.

Fast-forward eleven years: he had a GPA above 4.0, played elite basketball and made the varsity team in all four years of high school, set school athletic records, and scored exceedingly high on all tests. He never has been in trouble of any kind and listens to business podcasts for fun. He can't wait to get a job after college and even declined Division 1 university interest for basketball in lieu of trying for a business school of his choosing.

His younger sister, on the other hand, struggles in school, has various mental health challenges and learning disabilities. She has an immense passion for learning on her own. She is an expert on every type of government and reads manifestos for fun. She came out as gay when she was ten and changed her name when she was twelve. She plays guitar in a punk band and has her own thriving business, creating art and editing music videos. She shaves and/or dyes her hair and eyebrows, has several homemade (horrible) tattoos, and more than a few face piercings. And she has tens of thousands of followers on social media.

Both *mine*.

All for Nothing

From the time some people are kids, they start compiling a mental list of all the things they want for their own future kids; they think of the way they will do things, say things, and teach things to their future sons and daughters. Some of the listed items are based on wonderful experiences and ideas. Some are based on pain and disappointment or on a single interaction with their parents.

When we are expecting our children and then when they are perfect little beings who are totally helpless and pure, it is so much simpler to imagine how and when we will influence them, delight them, and show them the world in a beautiful way.

Then fast-forward to any given point at which they don't trust you enough to believe, for example, that they will get an upset tummy if they eat all of their Halloween candy. We start to see that this won't be like painting a masterpiece on a blank canvas, not at all.

We may even believe that all of the parents we've observed in our families or in fiction have been doing it wrong. We think it will go totally differently for us. We are sure of it. Cue all of the methods for forcing an outcome—the universe *loves* that!

Being effective—in other words, imparting the wisdom, teaching the lessons, and getting through to your teen—is based on your ability to be someone to whom they want to listen. Then, the next part is that even if they do believe what you're saying, how do you make sure they know that you are right and that, if they disagree, they are wrong?

There are so many possible side roads to take on the way to being effective. We must allow our teens to consider our vast wisdom and give them space to think and analyze whether or not they want to try it our way. It is counterintuitive, but we must use a light touch in sharing our views because if we apply pressure to a perfectly good view, that is the very thing they will revolt against. Teens want to see themselves as smart, independent, and capable, so we have to be a little bit more cool and a little bit less attached to whether or not they do it our way—the easier way, the best way—as their first choice.

Allowing our kids to have dignity and to build them up when they attempt to grow and figure things out is more important than their compliance to what we already know. Saying "I told you so" or "Why didn't you just listen to me?" are effectiveness-killers. The attitudes that spawn those comments are what keeps us at a distance and out of earshot of our kids when maybe they would be open to some advice.

Encouragement, mercy, optimism, belief, self-control, and kindness are what give us the open door to our teens' minds and hearts. If you want to be on the board of directors of the organization that is your teenager, you must be the kind of person to whom they want to listen and the kind of person they want to become.

The Black Hole

When I think back almost twenty years. when I taught high school, my first-period class comes to mind—mostly seniors, in their final semester of high school. I was getting discouraged, so I created an analogy that helped me to keep giving, loving, sharing, teaching, creating, motivating, and hoping. I didn't want to become numb or calloused or to lower my expectations, therefore reducing my input and passion. I might have self-combusted.

I just gave. I served it up, day after day. My all. My best work. All the love in my heart. All the jokes. All the fun. All the wisdom. Here it is: I pretended that my students were a black hole with a gravitational vortex. I remember reading somewhere that black holes actually drive the creation of galaxies. It clicked! I just blasted my best self with all my might, directed my energy toward the vortex, and believed in my heart that it would pay off. New galaxies would be created in their minds, even though I wouldn't see it in that moment or know it happened.

I taught to the tops of their heads while they slept or drooled on their desks and even when they seemed to be zoning out, chatting, or doing their math homework for second period instead of focusing on me.

And then, Facebook was invented. My students found me. I found some of them. Over and over, individually and without solicitation, they said things like this:

"Miss, I still have that quote you made for us on my mirror, and I've moved three times."

"Miss, you helped me so much. I always remember what you said that day in class."

"Miss, I decided to do something totally different than what my family expected me to do, and I followed my dreams because of that story you told me."

My jaw dropped. I hadn't known. I hadn't known that I had gotten through to them, but I had.

Parenting is like that. We try so hard, yet we see few or no results or even bad reactions to what we are trying to impart. It's hard to get up day after day and keep trying, keep serving it up, but I implore you (if that sounds serious, it is) to please stay charged up energetically. Keep your head on straight, and keep a thick skin so you don't get discouraged. Your teen's response in the moment is not an indicator of your effectiveness.

The more you flail around, thinking you're failing, the less your messages will get in their heads. You have to stay cool. The more insecure you are about your effectiveness, the less you'll try to be effective. You have to keep trying and have faith. It's all about trusting what you can't see. (Amen? Amen!)

Did You Hear That? It Sounded Like "Click"

They say babies have to try a new food up to twenty times before they like the taste. I think that's how it goes with new ideas, new techniques, and new levels of growth and maturity, from self-care to team work, from academic focus to attitude adjustments. I have worried so much that my hair is 40 percent gray, and I don't dye it so that I can keep track.

Then one day, out of nowhere—after I'd hung my head in defeat, betting on the fact that that child would never, ever put the toilet seat down, learn to wash their face, study for their tests, or put their plate in the freaking dishwasher—the angels started singing. First it was faintly, from a distance; then, the sweet falsetto hymns grew closer and closer, and tears formed in my eyes. I saw my child's mouth moving, and the sound that came clearly to my ears was, "Mom, I think I want to start working on that thing you are always telling me. I get it now." *Click.*

It clicked. Sometimes they don't say anything, especially when parents have been mean or righteous or harsh about the desired thing. It happens, though. Just this past week, one of mine came to me, after what I thought was a two-year delay in her tending to her hair, skin, odors, and changing clothes at least once a week, and said, "Mom, what soap should I use on my face at night? I want to start showering every day."

The thing here is to be graceful and *not* say, "Oh, God! Finally! I have told you this a million times! I told you I was right! Look at your zits! No wonder!" Dignity is a must here. We must be calm, cool, and honor their vulnerability, as they are making a change, improving their practices, and broadening their vision for what is possible in their future. It's a big deal, but *be cool.*

Also, we must follow their lead. Don't take their opportunity for growth and make it your new hobby by saying something like, "Wait! You said you'd do this now, and you didn't." Just let it unfold. Let it flow. It will happen. And even if it doesn't happen in your timing, remember that *is not* your problem. You have given them the information—hopefully, in a respectful way. Now, stop digging up the seeds you planted to see if they've sprouted!

Future Implications of Being Effective

Think back to my daughter who I said was not my type. What would have happened to her if I'd treated and parented her just like I treated her trouble-free, high-achieving brother?

What would have happened to our relationship if I had stayed firm in my idea that I was not right for her and that I would surely go crazy by trying to be her mom?

What if I had not resolved to grow, adapt, learn, and research and to put down my pride in service of actually showing up for her the way she needed me to?

What if I had made her wrong for not being like me, like her big brother?

What if I'd made her wrong for being wired like she is? For expressing herself like she does?

What if I'd chosen my preferences and ideals over actually meeting her needs?

What if I had blamed her for not getting with my program instead of creating a program that was the very best for who she actually is?

What if I'd given up because I didn't get what I wanted from her when I wanted it?

What if I didn't let her develop peacefully, with my constant support, and just harassed her continuously?

I am so glad I don't have to know what might have happened.

While people stare at this girl—half a foot taller than me, even without her Doc Martens—and judge us both, wrongly assuming she's a rebel or bad girl, we skip through the aisles of the grocery store, goofing around and enjoying the chance to be in each other's worlds.

I learn from her; she learns from me. We teach each other our points of view and our ways of understanding, learning, and seeing people and situations. I have become a better person—far more compassionate, adaptive, strong, humble, and gentle—because I told myself I was going to be the mom she needed me to be, not the mom I thought I was supposed to be. No one else had the honor of being her mom, so why would I need their approval?

I became the expert on this child, and the proof is evident. We have a healthy, fun, vital, open relationship that will last as long as we do. By the way, I am still super-close with my oldest son too, and I love that he has beautiful empathy and respect for his sister, his polar opposite, because he got to see me do it first.

I want you to think through the following questions:

- Do you try to parent the way you're "supposed" to parent, instead of how your gut tells you to respond to your teen?
- Do you give yourself room to experiment and figure out what's best for each of your kids?
- Have you ever asked your teen what they really need from you?
- Have you asked them about what you don't understand about them? Or what they wish you would understand about what it's like to be them?

Initiating these types of conversations can completely transform your relationship with your teenager.

Authentic

Authentic is a lot like being real, but I'm going to take it to a different place than you might expect. Let's look at authenticity from Brené Brown's perspective:

Authenticity is a collection of choices that we have to make every day. It's about the choice to show up and be real. The choice to be honest. The choice to let our true selves be seen.[1]

I Can't Find Myself Anywhere

As parents, it's easy to forget who are true selves are, much less let them be seen! Remember when you were cool? I help my clients, from eleven to seventy-two years old, to develop that *real* version of themselves, in full, vivid color, in terms of how they want to show up. Who do they show up as on vacation or after a glass of wine (for parents who enjoy alcohol, not the kids!), when all is well in the world? We work to harness that and apply that real, cool, authentic version of them to more areas of life—in parenting teens, in particular.

If who you really are is not remotely cool, that's okay! That's not the point here. Whatever or whoever you are—deep down, when no one is looking—that's the *you* for which we are searching. We conform, little by little. Ironically, we often start from when we were teenagers, although usually even younger, to what the world, our parents, our friends, or the people we want to accept us want us to be.

When we were little, we had a pure view of who we were. Sadly, it would be there still if our parents knew that it would work out if we were allowed to stay true to that pure self.

We change course because of something traumatic, or it could be just the slow drip of constant judgment and criticism. Sometimes it's a sharp, sudden turn away from our true selves, and sometimes it's a one-degree shift, one after another, until we feel lost and disconnected from the truth.

Who Am I?

Nothing is harder than parenting. *Nothing.* No one can convince me otherwise. From day one when I realized I was expecting a baby to year seventeen, month nine; from my "easiest" kid to my "hardest" kid, I have seen sides of myself I didn't know were there, for better or for worse. I have been challenged to change and grow in ways I could have done without. I have been at the lowest points of my life as a parent and the highest too.

The roller coaster is nauseating at times. I can't believe I'm still standing sometimes. And sometimes, I don't like what certain kids, certain personalities, or certain situations threaten or trigger inside of me. I don't like or relate to that person I am sometimes, but I have compassion for her. She is just trying to stay sane, to hold it together, and to not fail at this impossible job. I appreciate this fighter and problem-solver in me. I do, but I'm not sure she's always the best version of me for the parenting job that I have, twenty-four/seven. The pressure does not always expose my strengths; it's the exact opposite. I call this my *reactive me.*

I become what I call Vicious Vanessa—and to be clear, the main victim she loves to claw up is me. She has boundaries that keep her critical, mean, nasty, never good enough stuff to herself I suppose, but inside my head and heart, Vicious Vanessa says things like this to me: Why didn't you do better? Why is everything always wrong? Why are you not better? How can you destroy or violently fix everything?

I know better than to unleash this version of myself on my kids, but there are times when it takes everything I have to not lose it, especially when I'm tired, hungry, or overwhelmed or too many things are going wrong at once. I usually just shut down instead of lashing out, but either way, I'm not me, and what I'm doing is not working—not for my work, my kids, or my family—and internally, it can be a big mess.

What's your own version of that reactive, whoever-you've-become you? What stress, confusion, chaos, or fatigue has turned you into that "you," over time, on your worst days, even if it's just mostly in your head? It's the way you show up when you're rattled, and it may have become your default way of operating, just to keep things simple and stay on the defensive and "ready" position.

Let's name him or her. I love this quote by psychiatrist and author Daniel Siegel: "If you can name it, you can tame it!" The more you identify that your reactive self is not you, the more effective you can be in changing your behaviors and mindsets when dealing with your teenager.

Let's create an image or identity around who you really are.

- Who were you before you were a parent?
- What is the best of you?
- What have you lost sight of about yourself since becoming a parent?
- What do people love about you?
- What do *you* love about you?
- What are you most proud of yourself about? Think who you are, not what you've accomplished.
- What would you call this version of you?
- Do you miss her/him? Would your family like this version of you—the real you?

Name him/her too!

Mine is Very Vanessa. I'm *so* myself. I'm really fun, dorky, goofy, confident, bold, intense, compassionate, and energetic—and I'm all of those to a high degree. That is the actual me, and people respond to her, even kids—maybe especially kids!

The actual you doesn't have to be particularly awesome, by the way, but as kids get to be around ten years old or so, they start to sniff out our bullshit. So if we are being fake or inauthentic in some way—different from being real—then they sense that. It doesn't feel safe, so they start to lose respect for us.

Can you think of an example of that in your own childhood, when you saw the multiple sides of your parents and thought, *Wait! What? Who is that?*

We do need to put on different hats at different times, and there is a place and time for everything. At the core, however, what if you could flow from that place of confidence, knowing that, whatever comes your way, your best, actual self will handle it well, and that will be good enough?

Lots of authors, thinkers, teachers, and leaders talk about developing these types of personas to help increase self-awareness. Find a setup that you like, if this one isn't sticking.

Questions to Consider

- Have you lost yourself?
- Do you think it's possible to make space and time to be yourself?
- Do you know where to start?

(I like to think about Glennon Doyle's words from her memoir, *Love Warrior.* She wondered if she was just meant to fill a role in her life or to be a soul, with real dreams, wants, and desires.)

- Have you gotten so caught up in your never-ending, highly taxing role as parent that you are not sure what your soul is these days?

These are questions that only you can answer for yourself.
Let me ask some more:

- What is something you miss from before you were swallowed up whole by being a mom or dad or guardian?
- What is something you would love to do if you just had a break—something soul-soothing, something pure?
- Who can you share that with?

- Who would support you in creating this as a reality?
- Even if it's not immediate, can you start planning, saving, or scheming to give your soul a little bit of oxygen?

A liberated parent will be able to relate to, communicate with, and enjoy a teenager more than an ego-driven, suffering parent will.

Oh, the Irony

Teenagers have a beautiful way of reminding us what that freedom and confidence felt like. We may respond with jealousy, saying "I wish my parents had allowed me to be me," and then we subconsciously want to squash that freedom our teens feel—the freedom that we didn't get to experience.

We may resent our kids for having so much of what we didn't have, weren't allowed, or couldn't afford. I have met many parents who work tirelessly to provide a certain quality of life, safety, security, and freedom for their teenagers. Then, when their teenagers don't fall over themselves with grateful songs of praise and thanksgiving (which would honestly make me more suspicious than happy, most times), we are disappointed that perhaps we are perpetuating something in our kids that we don't stand for, like laziness, entitlement, being spoiled, and disregarding their things. I'm sure you can think of others.

Future Implications of Being Authentic

I came out as gay when I was thirty-eight. I'm forty-three now. I was married. Those five kids I keep telling you about were from seven to twelve years old. I asked for a divorce. After I told someone I got a divorce and why, she said, "*Oh no!* You were just such a cute couple!" She held her sad, extra-frowny face for a good ten seconds after she said it too. Imagine if I'd responded with, "I haven't checked our photos lately! You're right! We were a cute couple! That's a great reason to live an inauthentic life!"

The future implications of living a life that is not you—whatever that may mean to you specifically—are depressing, at best. I did think long and hard about staying in that marriage—'til death did we part—for the kids, despite feeling sad, frustrated, depressed, anxious, distracted, worried, unfulfilled, and misaligned.

Then I had a new thought, based on research that women typically outlive their husbands. I thought, *Maybe when he passes on to be with Jesus, I will meet a cute lesbian like me at Bunko or at the assisted-living facility, and we will date!* I was genuinely excited for this future of mine. If I could wait out five babies times—forty-five months of pregnancy in sixty months—then I could surely wait for this too.

Then I thought that the kids would say, upon meeting my new sweetheart, "Mom! You're *gay*?"

To which I would have to answer in the affirmative.

They'd say, "When did you first know?"

And I would reply, "When I was eight, twelve, sixteen, eighteen, twenty-two—um, yeah, pretty much forever I've known."

To which they would say, "Why did you wait so long? Why did you marry Dad? Why did you stay with him? Why did you just now get to be who you are at the age of eighty-one?"

To which I would say, "I didn't want to hurt you guys by divorcing your dad."

And they would say, "So, instead, you decided to live a lie and be sad, frustrated, depressed, anxious, distracted, worried, unfulfilled, and misaligned while trying to raise us to be the opposite of those things?"

I chose authenticity. I chose to make a bold move. I chose to model courage. I chose to bet on my belief in their love for me and my ability to keep being a committed parent to them, regardless of whether I was married to their father. I knew it would hurt them to see us part and to feel the pain of the breakup and the fallout that truly does last for years. I also knew, however, that they would benefit (more than they would be hurt by the divorce) from watching their mom be who she is, living free and brave.

I have had multiple, individual private conversations with my kids—from back then up to as recently as this week—in which they honor me in some way for marrying my wife, being so happy, doing what was right for me, not letting my faith keep me pent up, embracing God's love for me, and so on. I've even been a topic of three different language arts assignments.

If there is an area of your life in which you're hiding something real and true about yourself, even to yourself, please come out with it—you don't need anyone's permission. Is it about your job? Is it about your marriage? Is it about your home? Is it about a feeling? A desire? Please tell someone. You can google me if you don't know anyone else who's safe to tell. I'll listen!

Loving

If I could pick one thing for you to leave with after reading this book, it would be to understand, to a fuller and deeper extent, what love is. (Oh, how insulting!) I know you know what love is, but for a moment, take the perspective that you don't. Just pretend you're three years old. You've heard someone say, "I love you," and you've said, "I love ice cream and puppies," for as long as you remember, but what *is* it, exactly?

Order the Following Book Right Now

I read a book that changed my life and my perspective on love forever. A dear friend and fellow master coach recommended it to me. (Thank you, Kristeen.) It's called *Loveability: Knowing How to Love and Be Loved* by Robert Holden, PhD. I've recommended it to numerous people who have thanked me profusely.

Here's what I learned—and trust me: a part of my five-decades-plus self *did not like* learning this!

I do not need to *do* anything to earn my own or other's love and approval. If it's something I'm working for or walking the line to keep, it is not love. It's something else.

Judgment is not love. I am in this amazing space where judgment does not come up as one of my options anymore. I'm still savvy and have opinions and think, but I have realized that when I judge myself (my all-time favorite former hobby) and my family and others, it just fills the space completely. When I choose judgment, I have decided that my approval is more important than their inherent right to be accepted and understood.

Also, Dr. Holden introduced me to this quote that John Steinbeck wrote in *East of Eden*: "The greatest terror a child can have is that he is not loved, and rejection is the hell he fears."

We don't mean to reject our kids, but when we do, it's like death by a thousand cuts. We must lead with love and acceptance of our teens, again creating the safe space they need to open up, to know we are there, and to keep our ego and fears at bay.

I recommend that you read or listen to *Loveability* as soon as possible. It will free you up immensely and allow you to understand yourself in a new way—and therefore have access to the most unconditional, loving version of you, one you may have not met yet. (Order it now. I'll wait.)

Fear Is Futile

All parents say, "Of course I love my child!" It's a no-brainer. Of course, but I'd like to dig into this one: Do you approve of your child? Do you feel it's your place to decide if what they like, think about, look like, and desire for their future is a yes or a no? I'm not talking about addiction or harmful, life-altering activities. I'm talking about style, experiments, explorations—the way a person operates as they bravely try to figure out their identity and their gifts and passions in life. Do you have lots of guidance and wisdom to offer that's just a thinly veiled fear that they will fail, suffer, not be accepted, or not be loved (by others and/or you)?

This is where we must separate our fears from our parenting. I swear they give us an invisible, five-ton bag of fears to hold on to forever when they hand us our children. It's difficult to differentiate fear from parenting. Let's play some of the tape that might run through the minds of parents, especially when they are about to turn out kids into the real world. The pressure is on.

"What if they can't feed themselves? What if their roommate hates them because they are lazy and dirty? What if they never buy themselves deodorant? What if they never figure out how to be on time or wake up on their own? What if they think that social media is real life? What if people think I failed because they aren't going to college? What if they never realize their potential? What if no one loves them because they are _____. What if they can't support themselves? What if they attach themselves to the wrong people? What if they hurt themselves or others because they think they're invincible? What if they aren't happy? What if they can't survive in the big, mean world?"

What if, what if, what if? All of these questions are based in fear (or reality—if that's how your mind wants to see it).

Our very best chance of putting these questions and their answers to rest is to completely turn away from *what if* (that is, all the bad things that are based on fears and the not-measuring-up ideas) and turn to *love*. Turn toward support. Turn toward being present, toward waking up. Turn to being involved, to understanding, and to accepting people for who they are and being patient while they find their way (as they inevitable will). And I do mean *their* way, not your way.

More on the Clicking

The daughter I told you about earlier said for years that she didn't want to go to college; she even said she didn't want to finish high school, on and off. I just listened; I got why she was saying that. She didn't drop out. That's not something I felt was a solution because I could hear that high school wasn't the actual problem. It was something deeper about her self-image and the way she saw her future self. I just held space and did not force the issue or try to convince her, motivate her, manipulate her, or bribe her to choose college, which was not easy for me because college was amazing for me. I loved school. I rocked school, and I also saw that she was capable and would thrive in higher education. It was a better fit for her than high school.

Then, one day, not too long ago, she started saying things like, "When I graduate high school," and "When I go to college, I want to do this and that," and "When I'm a teacher," and so on. I was sure not to say, "Oh good, you realized I was right. Thank God!" And I didn't shame her for her previous stance on her education and job prospects. I kept myself in check and just said, "How exciting! How does that feel?" I started to jump on to *her* vision for her future. It turned out to align with mine, so that was great for me, I guess, but think about this: how likely would she be to *want* to go my way if I was forcing it upon her?

Dust This Book Off or Reorder It Now

A book by Gary Chapman from 1992 called *The Five Love Languages* has been a particularly useful tool for my family and for my clients too. He wrote several other books that relate to the concept of love languages—for children, teens, singles, etc. *The Five Love Languages of Teenagers: The Secret to Loving Teens Effectively* is a powerful book. You can find out your love language and those of everyone in your family with quizzes found on his website. I send the link, from time to time, to my kids and wife. The five love languages are words of affirmation, physical touch, acts of service, quality time, and gifts. If you know what language is your main one (or two) and what your teenager's is also, you can gain an entire universe of information that has the potential to answer dozens of questions you've yet to answer on why the way you express love doesn't seem to get through to your teenager. You also can see that the things teens say and do are their ways of trying to show you their love. Go to town on this, but go with an open mind. You should approach every suggestion, situation, and conversation with a sense of curiosity, an absence of judgment, and hope for change and new possibilities.

I recently coached a mom on this tool. Her daughter, thirteen, seemed to appreciate receiving gifts as her preferred demonstration of love, but the mom did not score gifts high at all. In fact, receiving gifts was her least preferred method, so there was a great risk of her believing that her daughter was shallow and materialistic. This was the cause of much of their tension and screaming matches. The mom didn't feel appreciated for what she did or tried to do because it didn't translate as love to the daughter. When she learned her daughter's love language was related to receiving gifts, the mom automatically thought, *Wow, this is going to be expensive.* After we broke it down, though, she realized that she could do little things and actively search for ways to show her daughter, in a tangible way, that she was thinking of her. It could be a flower from the garden, a snack-size Snickers, or a thoughtful purchase at the grocery store.

She had to open her mind to accept that her daughter was most likely to feel and understand how much she meant to her mom in ways that simultaneously did not mean that much to her mom, if the tables were turned. The mom, on the other hand, really needed quality time with her daughter to experience a sense of connection and affection, so she started focusing more on creating these opportunities, like having shows that were just for them to watch—no siblings, no dad. She realized, to her delight, that giving her girl the gift of her time and presence was a close match for what made her girl feel loved too.

Future Implications of Being Loving

I have dozens of stories like this that I have experienced with my own eyes and ears—kids being in complete opposition to their parents, even when they want the same thing. The moral here is that we have to relax, let kids figure things out, be nearby in case they need help, and be safe, open, and available but not leave them feeling the high-stakes pressure of needing to measure up in order to eventually be someone their parents or others will approve of or love fully.

I bring us back now to being *loving*. Gentle. Flexible. Unattached to outcomes, focused on effort and consistently showing up in a "REAL" and "CLEAN" way for our kids.

You can't give someone something that you don't have, so if you have a surplus of reasons why you love yourself—because you lost weight, got a job, made money, looked the part, measured up, got the "likes," were told you're great, etc.—then you might need to do some digging. If all of that went away—*poof*—would you still love yourself the same? Minus all of the conditions that you've worked hard to create in your life, do you love *you*, the little you who has nothing to show for yourself but who you are?

If you have a deficit of love, approval, kindness, openness, flexibility, understanding, and compassion for yourself, then this is your cue. First, read *Loveability*! I don't care if you love it or hate it. Just read it to the end, and see what you think, and then be awake to the fact that once you are sure that you know what love is, you can proceed with confidence that you can give that to your teenager.

REAL Summary

People faking being real seems really popular right now. People say they are being vulnerable just to illicit a certain response. Also, *real* can be used as an excuse to be mean, harsh, or judgmental, as in, "I'm just keeping it real."

When you think of being real, I invite you to remember the acronym REAL and focus on being *r*esilient, *e*ffective, *a*uthentic and *l*oving. There is nothing wrong with you, no matter what you've been brainwashed to believe.

One time, when working with an intense, amazingly driven

woman, I said, "I just want you to know that I figured out what is wrong with you."

She said, "Oh no!" and then, "Oh great! I've always wanted to know!"

I waited. I paused as long as I possibly could. I built it up and up and finally said, "Lady, the only thing wrong with you is that you think something is wrong with you."

We laughed so hard we almost cried.

You can be you. You can be real. You are naturally resilient. You are naturally going to find out how to find stuff out, figure out what you don't know, and try a hundred times to be effective until you are—if you have the courage to be real. You can let your hair down and strip down to the truth, with nothing false to hide what's totally, truly for you—and you will be okay. You will not just survive that, but you'll end up with a subsequent deep-cleaning opportunity for your life that will allow you to purge all that is not a fit for your truth. You can be loving, unafraid, full-hearted, without excuses, and not fear-loving as a result.

Real is the basis of functioning in life and functioning with your teenager as well, as you know you can. Real is the new black. Real is the deal. Real is the answer. Real is the thing you are going to be required to get real with if you're going to be the one who makes the biggest difference in your relationship with your teen.

Now, go tell someone something real about you, and then watch while your heart might feel like it's pounding out of your chest, how it will keep beating, and you will feel more alive than you ever have. I'll wait.

Part 3
CLEAN

If each of us would only sweep our own doorstep,
the whole world would be clean.
—Mother Teresa

Better keep yourself clean and bright; you are the
window through which you must see the world.
—George Bernard Shaw

What Does Operating CLEAN Look Like?

What would your life be like tomorrow if you were sure that you could manage your life while being connected to yourself and your needs; if you were levelheaded and wise about whatever came your way, expressive to those you love and to yourself about a job well done and places you could grow, aware of the beauty and realness around you, genuinely grateful, and nice—just kind and gentle to yourself, realizing that you're not going to make or break anything by being a bully.

Clean is the goal. Think about eating clean, clean fuel, clean living, no dirt under the rug, no bullshit—just pure and solid clean in the design, in the details, and in the day-to-day. This is the way it is with my teens and me.

I want to tell you how it is for me with these five teenagers—as of this writing (2020), they are ages twelve, thirteen, fifteen, sixteen, and eighteen. Each one is more different than the next. The two boys live with their dad, primarily. I talk to them almost every day. They answer my calls, Facetime, and texts when they are playing golf, Xbox—you name it. And it's not because I get mad or sad if they don't. They see my contact picture pop on their phones, and they know I'm going to be real—things are clean; there's no drama, no agenda. We each can say what we need to say and be how we need to be. There's a real connection that is bigger than how many minutes we spend on the phone. If a few days go by, we are never concerned. They want to spend time with me. It's real, not an obligation; it's not contrived.

When they each decided to live with their dad full time, I was their biggest supporter because I genuinely want them to have what they need in their lives. And if that's less mom and more dad, then good. We know that our relationship is real, and it's not based on proximity or who makes them dinner. It's not based on anything but love—and never selfishness. We each get to say when we want to hang out, which is plenty, and they feel fine saying, "I'm good," and pushing to another day if I'm the initiator. There's freedom and respect.

My three girls live with me primarily but split time with their dad. People sometimes say with three girls, "Oh the drama," but we don't see it like that. There is an attitude of kindness, peace, fun, and openness around our house. They come to me and to each other when they struggle and when they are happy. They help in the house. You may not believe it, but we don't yell, roll our eyes, or slam doors here.

Last week, I was trying to finish something (probably part of this book) and the delivery person came with the groceries (COVID's new normal). I texted one girl to bring the groceries in and to please put them away. I told her to please get her two younger sisters if she needed help. I was down the hall and could hear the whole thing unfolding. First of all, they were all glad to help. They didn't ask why or where I was. Second, they laughed and helped each other with the stuff, dividing up parts of the job. One offered to another, "Go ahead back to your game. I can get the rest done." And I thought, *Wow!*

I'm obviously not one to take this stuff for granted. Quite the opposite! When my sixteen-year-old came in to tell me they were done with the job, I told her that I'd heard them interacting, and I acknowledged her leadership, saying that it was so beautiful to listen to them in the kitchen.

I asked, "Do you think you guys are like that because of how I treat you, or what?"

Then she said—and I'm not making this up, even though math is not her gift, and she's spent a lifetime avoiding it, and even though it was so beyond clever and insightful that you might not believe that a teenager said it—"Yeah. I think that's why. We are just like you, but squared."

Like Mom^2! I said, "Shut up! That is brilliant! Did you make that up? Is that a thing already, or was that your idea?" (After giving my son credit for a hilarious joke that he passed off as original writing, which actually was verbatim from a meme, they know I now ask for sources.)

What an amazing idea. Whatever way we choose to show up in life, whether that is MEAN or CLEAN, what if our teens became the equivalent of MEAN times MEAN or CLEAN times CLEAN? We reckon with the fact that there is a high correlation to how we operate, speak, act, and think with how our teens are influenced by the whole of that, no matter what we say to ourselves to blame them for their problems. Do you want teenagers who take full responsibility for their actions and inactions? Okay then but we, the parents, have to go first!

Math review. If you are MEAN^1, then they are MEAN^1. Not bad. But if you are MEAN^2, then they are MEAN^4. If you are MEAN^{10}, then they are MEAN^{100}. Same deal with REAL and CLEAN too!

It feels weird to say this because it makes me sound like I'm full of shit, but I want to give you a glimpse of what is possible when you value CLEAN over MEAN. Would you like to see where your possible blind spots are? I'll show you, if you're not too busy rolling your eyes about me and my fake teenagers.

Here we go!

Connected
Levelheaded
Expressive
Aware
Nice

Connected

When we seek connection—not approval, not enabling, not codependency, not people-pleasing but real connection, human-to-human compassion, seeking to understand one another, wanting to meet each other's needs and caring about relationships over order, power, and optics—we get to walk a much smoother, healthier path together as parents and teens.

Get a Passport and Get in Their World

My teens have varied interests, different from each others' and from my own, yet I find ways every day to let them know I'm in their world. I don't stay connected so I can get the dirt on them, but I do get a lot of good intel when we talk and share time together. Lying on a couch, on the floor, or in bed together is probably where I get the best connections for my kids and me. I come in, sit down, and ask what's up. I bring no agenda, and I don't talk about a dish or some clothes here and there. I just am *with* them. I ask questions about a video, a game, a friend, a project, or a teacher. Again, this is not for a real purpose, just out of true curiosity, because I want to understand what it's like to be them. I also want them to *see* that I care, not just hear me say I care.

Many times, I get very little, and everything is boring and dull. Other times, I get a river of feelings, thoughts, ideas and plans, fears and insecurities, victories, anxieties, hope, and disappointments.

I'll play the odds. I know if I keep coming back, and they know that my ratio of just being with them versus complaining, criticizing, bossing them around, or nagging them is at least five to one, I will get to the one time when they open up to me and allow me to contribute to them. I will play the odds, even if they only open up to me on one-fifth of my visits!

What Do You Think?

Another way I connect with my teens is to ask their opinions—on the phone, in person, or in passing, very frequently. I tell them what I'm dealing with, how I'm feeling, when I have a win, when I have a loss, when my energy is low, when I feel stuff, when something is driving me crazy, or when I can't figure something out. I like to share with them and give them a glimpse into the fact that I am human too. I'm not a mom-bot. I'm not a perfect person. I model this, and it gives them a chance to contribute to me too.

If you ask genuine questions of your teens and listen to what they have to say, as if they are trusted advisers, I promise that you often will be surprised by the astute insights a teenager can offer. I want to drill this into the collective head of the world: teenagers are smart, and they understand a lot more than most people believe they do. They see things in a simple way that is very clever and wise. I see this in my teen clients and in my own kids, every single day. I observe this in kids with whom I work and whose parents have told me that their teen is "not all there." Just a reminder: you will always find what you are looking for in a person.

Case 1 for Meditation

You need to find a way to try, practice, and/or ramp up your ability to connect with yourself. I know, with 100 percent certainty, that learning to breathe and meditate, to connect with yourself, to get into your own world, to ask yourself what you think, to clear out the garbage, to get in touch with your higher power or positive energy will be worth it. All of the answers you need are inside of you. I'm serious—you might have known everything I've written in this book if you had just meditated. Doesn't that make sense? Maybe that's because you already knew! By the way, the more REAL you are, the easier it is to connect with yourself. No one's fake self wants to connect with anyone.

Future Implications of Being Connected

A few side effects of building a connection with your teens through asking them their opinions (and not arguing or shutting them down when they do) is that they will experience themselves as smart, trusted, capable, and confident. They also will see that it's okay to ask you for your opinion when they have something going on. You model vulnerability. You model open-mindedness.

We must stop acting like it's a mystery why teens are so closed-minded, hard-headed, think they know everything, and never listen, when maybe it's because no one ever showed them what that looks like. Maybe they are just doing what you're doing. It may not be the case, but it's a good place to look when you're frustrated with your teen.

Levelheaded

When we are tempted to operate from fear, distrust, or worst-case scenarios, we can seem unreasonable. We throw out facts and compromise; we forget about teaching. Patience is not even in the building. We lose our ability to be understood, heard, or effective.

Insanity, Solved

I had a client who was a single dad of a fourteen-year-old boy. He was extremely frustrated and so angry that he could hardly see straight because his kid could not get his schoolwork organized, completed, and turned in on time. He yelled. He punished. He raged. He forced his son to do manual labor at sunrise. He threatened him with losing basically everything that wasn't nailed down. Once, he even said to me (and I've heard this more than once) that he would take away his breath if he could, if it would make a difference. It was as a joke, of course, but this was all to say that he obviously cared about his son's academic habits and success, but he was out of options for how to "make" him perform. I worked with the son, mostly, but after one session, I invited the dad to have a quick conversation with me.

I asked him if he knew what he would want if the tables were turned. I asked him what was missing in his approach with his son and his school struggles. He knew immediately.

He said, "Oh, my God. He just needs help. He needs me to help him, doesn't he?"

A switch flipped. They became partners. They sat side by side and worked out what he was missing in all of his classes. They created a list, and together, they started kicking this list's butt together. The dad sat nearby, coached his son, and answered questions as his son plowed through his work. To think that their relationship actually had a chance to improve by solving problems together was surprising to them both. It was not easy for the father to refrain from blaming his son for this mess, just a few weeks from the end of the quarter, and for the stress it caused him, but the dad figured that if he could take off an afternoon for happy hour or golf, then he could do the same to sit beside his son and create a new partnership with him. You can see that the results—the son raising his grades from D's and F's to C's and B's—was not the big win here, right?

After our next meeting, the dad said, "We are building something really cool for his science project, so we have to head to the hardware store from here."

The boy pulled out the list from his pocket. They put their arms around each other's shoulders, walked out like the buddies that they had always wanted to be for each other, and headed to Ace Hardware.

You're Making It Harder than It Needs to Be

Being levelheaded is harder to do in some ways because we have to give up a lot of our opinions and judgments and just deal with what's happening. Being levelheaded is easier in some ways too because it's like skipping the middleman—to go from an issue at hand to the solution, like making it from point A to point B without having to go through points G, K, W, and L which makes no sense at all, but is what anger can do to us all.

What does it take to not be triggered all day, every day, by the myriad predictable and unexpected stimuli we face as parents of teens? Any ideas?

I have a few! Let's talk about mindfulness. Let's talk about getting a grip. Let's talk about lengthening our fuses and creating a buffer between our lowest self and variables A through Z that come our way daily. Reactivity—like anger, sarcasm, mocking, critical jabs, passive-aggressive tactics, and power-grabs—is *not* being levelheaded.

Levelheadedness comes from a sense of peace, confidence, security, and trust. If you believe you have skills that work, even in sticky situations, you will learn to rely on this calm foundation and show up for yourself and your teen in a way that works.

Imagine any other job in which the variables come at you, and you are not able to get grounded or make pragmatic and sound decisions while the other side of the equation (boss, customer, client, patient) at least understands and respects you for your point of view. That is generally grounds for firing, and since being fired as a parent is uncommon, we have to get this aspect of ourselves in charge— even when it comes to our relationships with teenagers.

Case 2 for Meditation

If you want access to that level head that you know is in there, you will have to get out of fight-or-flight mode, which means the sympathetic division of your autonomic nervous system is on fire, like you're being chased by the DEA with a trunk full of drugs. You are on high alert because life is so crazy, and the truth is that that's just how life is occurring for you. It's not true; it's your perception. Then you believe that perception of chaos and react to it. You fight. You walk out. You slam the door. You yell. You get tense. You try to calm down by doing things that are addictive and harmful. Even if this is on a small scale for you, I invite you to get a grip on it.

To get started on meditation with a friendly helper (the applications' calming voices), please download an app like Calm or Headspace (some versions are free), and start with baby steps, like two or three minutes. There are a zillion guided meditations on YouTube. Look around 'til you find one you like, and let someone teach you via your phone.

Your parasympathetic division of your autonomic nervous system, which is the rest and digest piece, when allowed to be activated, will allow you to have a buffer from stress. You will feel grounded, still, and peaceful. You may come away fter just a few minutes in this mode of breathing with answers to problems, having let yourself release stress. You will have access to actual wisdom and perspective.

Future Implications of Being Levelheaded

This levelheaded thing is a by-product of figuring out what underlies our irrational and illogical, counterproductive behavior; subsequent feelings; and the destructive results they cause. You may find out through using therapy, counseling, coaching, a mental health evaluation, a hormone check, a recovery program, a timeout, or energy work. You need to do whatever it takes to find out why you lose it when life is happening, maybe every time. I didn't need to tell you this; you already knew. Please take this as a nudge. It's time.

If you're not ready to get to the underlying cause yet, then at least pursue proper self-care and exercise, and share with someone you trust about what you're dealing with. The more vulnerable you can get, the more headway you'll make. It's going to be hard, but it will be worth it. Getting help—medical, psychological, professional help—is not something you'll ever regret. (You might find out you're perfect, and it's the whole world's fault, and it would then be official! Maybe you can get a certificate!)

Expressive

Most of us have heard of or experienced a relationship between parent and child in which the parent never says "I love you." It's sad to hear and even sadder to understand the way the child would justify the lack of expression of affection and endearment. We naturally want to make it okay for people we love when they don't show up as fully as we need them to do. Let's not make our teens have to do that for us, okay?

Mind if I Take a Look?

You have the opportunity to check in with yourself to see if:

1. you are holding back the explicit words that your teen needs to hear;
2. you have a block about being expressive (which you can seek to discover and create a strong new awareness of); and/or
3. there are baby steps you can take to start the work of saying what you mean and meaning what you say to your teenager.

Stay the same as you were before you read this book, if you'd like, but I will show you new options; it's your choice to apply them or not.

Let's Take a Trip Down Memory Lane

One quick way into this realm of expression is to think about the most impactful words anyone ever said to you. Let's look at positive examples first.

Who said those words?

What did those positive words spark inside of you?

What was the impact on your choices? Self-concept? Mood? Actions? Thoughts?

Now let's look at the most hurtful words. This is harder, but it may be more memorable. Think of one comment, assumption, judgment, or criticism that you've heard or read about yourself that just really stung.

Ironically, it could be something your teenager said to you or about you. How many years, months, or days did that mess you up?

What about things people have said you to that were kind and supportive, but they said them to manipulate you?

Now think of anything you regret saying to someone, your teen or otherwise, that you know had a negative impact.

Words, both said and unsaid, are powerful. They can give us a new possibility for our lives, or they can leave us with pain, especially when we believe the lies someone said are true.

In having a clean, fully functional relationship with our teenagers, we need to seek to have a one-to-one ratio of our words matching our real selves, our true hearts. Nothing more; nothing less.

Words of affirmation are not always the most important part of the relationship for everyone, but they don't hurt.

What are five things you want to say to your teen that you know would make a difference if *you* said them?

Here are some examples:

- Acknowledge something you saw in them.
- Show respect for something they did.

- Say something complimentary about their character.
- Express interest in their interest.
- Say how you feel about them.
- Tell them how you are inspired by them.

Why? Why? Why?

Another aspect of expression is not requiring people to understand you when you don't seek to be understood or don't do the work to be understood. So many opportunities for misunderstandings and assumption-making happen when we don't have the courage or take the time to explicitly tell someone not only what we want and need but why.

What is one thing that you want and need from your teenager that they do not comply with. Have you ever told them the reason why you need it? Do you even know the real reason why?

Let's do an exercise together. Choose a topic regarding a want or need currently in your life, but the request hasn't proven effective.

What is it? I'll show you mine: I want my kids to take initiative with cleaning the dishes.

The obvious reason why is that they dirtied them, and no one should have to clean up after anyone else.

Now let's go deeper. Why else does it matter to me? Because I am not free all day anymore to clean up. I work. I don't have the time available to do that, as well as taking care of my self-care and larger responsibilities.

What's another reason? I don't want them to be the worst roommates and spouses on earth or to have bugs and flies in their homes.

Another? I want them to care about the people who share space with them, and for some reason, someone cleaning their dishes represents that.

Why is that? Because if they turn out bad, lazy, or selfish, then

I must have failed at parenting. And if that's true—well, I would deem myself as worthless, I guess.

So wow. Dishes are a heavy topic after all. Imagine if there were burned-on, crusty pots and not just a plate with a dab of cream cheese on it.

What becomes possible if I remove all of the heaviness from the chore? What if they have no idea that I associate this thing about my worthiness in being a good mom with their cereal bowl on the end table?

I could either be vulnerable and tell them why I get so weird about dishes, or I can deal with myself about my self-esteem issues— or both.

Your turn.

Can you see how expressing yourself, both to yourself (looking deeper within) and sharing with your teen about why you "make a big deal" about this or that or everything could make a difference in your relationship?

Just Say It

We want to be able to say what's true for us when our feelings are hurt, when we are worried that our kids won't need us anymore, when we are concerned about a possible trend we are observing, or when we want to spend time with our teen or by ourselves. We also want to say what's true for us when we are proud of our kids or when we want them to know that we have always known they would figure something out.

A lot of talking without communicating happens between parents and teens. Talking about logistics, chores, school, odors, appearances, and screen time can easily take up 90 percent of the bandwidth or air time that our teenagers allot us.

What would happen if you led with, focused on, and prioritized genuine conversations over the nagging kind? Is it possible that you're stuck in a cycle, and you're the only one who can stop it?

Did you just think, *No! If they do the things they are supposed to do, that will stop the cycle of nagging and underperformance?* Maybe, but we could try something new since the old thing is not working as it "should."

When your kids see *Mom* on their phones or messages, or when they see your face or hear your car pull up, do they think, *Yes! I want to tell her something cool or get her help with something I'm stuck on!* Or do they just ignore you because your script is so predictable—something they've heard a hundred thousand times? Or do they avoid you because you're scary and critical from the second you walk in the door, searching for the people while simultaneously searching for all things undone and wrong things in the house.

Make a list of ten things you can talk about that are not predictable to your teen. Get going. Just try it. Let's see what happens when you intentionally communicate with them and then listen to them when they communicate about things that aren't forever being said, like a skipping CD from 1995.

When they trigger you and all the deeper meanings behind your overreactions, what is something you can say to yourself to gain perspective and be a more effective communicator?

Case 3 for Meditation

The difference between expressing yourself or not lies in the answer to this question: If I dare to express myself, will anyone listen?

Meditation is an opportunity for you to be quiet and calm the clutter in your mind, even for a few minutes; get access to your true feelings and thoughts; and increase clarity. Why would your mind waste its time doing something like think great thoughts about you, your future, or your family if all you have time for are the things that need to be controlled, fixed, handled, researched, planned, and complained about. Why would your mind come out of its little hole and tell you anything important—like what you really feel, what you really want, or what you really need—if you are always telling it to shut up and go back to its dark little hole so you can pour some wine?

Don't get mad at me. Drink your wine! I'm just saying that I want you to make time to be with yourself too, fully sober from all external sources—from technology, other people, all the inputs and pulls of life. I want you to listen to yourself, to trust what you hear, and to act on what you know, deep down.

Future Implications of Being Expressive

Here's how I see humans.: We are here on this planet at the exact time and for the exact duration for an exact reason. Our only job is to express ourselves fully, freely, and with confidence that we will make the difference that we need to make.

When my time is finished, there is no doubt that when I look back on my life, I'll want to be sure that I didn't leave anything unsaid and that what I did say to my kids were the exact things that made a difference in their lives. I want to be sure that they can see—in the way I expressed all of me, my thoughts, my gifts, my talents, my passions, and my feelings—that I was proud of who I was and how I lived my life.

All of that comes down to my expression. It matters that we learn how to express ourselves in the most effective, inspiring way possible.

Aware

It's very common in my coaching practice for parents to come to me with one objective or problem to solve. Then, when I speak with the kid, I find out that the parent is mistaken about the actual issue. They are often hyper-focused on something that is minor, compared to what is the kid's reality. That's not a spot in which we, as parents, want to find ourselves. The access to awareness is connection, plus a level head.

If You're Scary, No One Wants to Talk to You

If your teen can count on you to come at a mistake or an issue with a level head, and they trust that you are truly connected to them (the fullness of who they are, not just their merits and results in life), then you will be in the know.

Awareness and numbness (from MEAN in part 1) are probably the most counterproductive to the principles we are learning here.

What do you focus on the most? Probably some combination of work, self-care (hopefully), and family, figuring out food and rides, homework help, deadlines, and so on.

All of those are things to do, and they are necessary, *but* justifying that there is so much going on and being in a chronic state of being overwhelmed is not conducive to being parents who are aware of what their teens are feeling, thinking, and doing.

It's okay if you're not there yet with this one. It's challenging, for sure. I am asking you to look at which parts of life you get caught up in that reduce your ability to pick your head up and see what is going on around you.

Life360

I'm going to be a little on the controversial side of something right now. Installing apps for tracking your kids' every move, like Life360, does not make you an aware or connected parent. Sure, you get lots of ammo—many of your fears may be confirmed or denied, or you'll feel a sense of security and a right to know. Keep in mind, though, that I have not coached one kid who is on that app who doesn't know how to hack it, beat it, and outsmart you.

What if you took the energy that is required for monitoring your kids and just worked hard, here with me, to become a safe space for them to share the actual 360 degrees of their lives? We can agree to disagree here, but I can tell you it is very difficult to create a respectful relationship, one based on dignity and trust, when we are tracking our kids like the FBI. It's another example of trying to force outcomes or to take shortcuts where we could be creating a real foundation for openness and communication.

If you love Life360 and it gives you peace, go for it, but please consider using it in tandem with your child, versus a "gotcha" tactic, as a tool for justifying punishment, or in place of real relationship.

Hello, It's Your Wake-Up Call!

Another caveat of parenting is not making the space for kids to come out and tell you something. I have heard many kids say, "I've been trying to tell them about this, but all they talk about or care about are my grades, and this is way bigger."

We have access to our teens' grades, longitude and latitude, how many hard brakes they made in traffic, their phone history, and so on. I call these the metrics, but having a 100 percent grasp of all of those facts and figures is not a replacement for communication and understanding what they are dealing with.

Just like money doesn't automatically make people happy, perfect grades do not indicate that a teenager is happy either. There is not a one-to-one relationship between performance and optics and the truth of what is happening with your teen. It could be anything from self-esteem to self-harm, addiction, an abusive relationship, mental health issues, perfectionism, self-induced pressure, suicidal thoughts and/or plans, or misunderstandings that shape their view of the world, the family, and you.

Two of the biggest blocks to being aware of what our kids are going through and dealing with are (1) thinking we already know what is going on and (2) preaching about how it was for us when we were young, instead of being acutely interested in what it's like to be them now.

The Guillotine

Awareness is a good thing, even when you become aware of something you didn't want to happen. Teens feel very isolated in today's world.

There's a universal thing going on: teens present the appearance of having many friends and a great family, but they feel that they have no one to whom they can turn.

I have an image in my head of teenagers, each being alone in a dark room, looking down, with just a faint light glowing from their screens. They look up to see a scrolling ticker lit up on the wall, going around and around, faster and faster, with all of the comments and cruelness they have read about themselves or their friends. They are fearful of being exposed or of someone making fun of them for any wrong move. They look behind them and see faces peering in their windows, spying, waiting to embarrass or bully them. Then they look across the room and see the door. It leads to their parents, but even though it's hell in the teens' own space, alone, they imagine telling their parents, making them aware of what it's like, why they are angry a lot, why they don't want to have fun like before, why they have been distant, and they realized it's not that simple. They hesitate; if they think that they will be punished for struggling or messing up, it won't be worth the risk to share. Maybe they picture the hallway between their door and yours being rigged with booby traps and maybe even a guillotine, waiting to destroy them for the very thing that is causing their pain, shame, and fear.

Sounds dramatic, I know, but I get enough of the inside scoop to know that the people that teens want to tell the most are not the safest place to turn. In reality, parents would be the best choice, but in our teens' minds, it's not the case. *How will Mom handle me wanting to tell her I'm vaping/cutting/failing math if she freaks out every time I don't close the door quietly or forget my uniform at home?* Not perfect logic, but it's teen logic, in many cases.

Instead of teaching them to do better, having a great talk, getting it off their chest, and creating a plan for change and accountability, they have to be punished—stripped of privileges.

There are infinite opportunities for growth that parents trade in, callously and blindly, by yanking electronics, car keys, and going-out rights from their teens.

Case 4 for Meditation

Meditation is the tool for creating self-awareness. If you're not self-aware, then how can you be aware of anyone else and be accurate in your assessment? If you're not self-aware, then how can you feel confident in what you're doing and how you're relating to and leading your teenager?

On the other hand, if you are able to tap into your wisdom and be aware of what you may not be aware of, what could you see or sense? What would you say? How would that wisdom impact your teenager? What if you could model self-awareness, teaching your teenager to go within and calm down all the racket to see what's there and what needs to be done.

I love coaching because so much of its power comes from asking people great questions. I wouldn't be able to ask the best, most insightful questions, Socrates-style, if I wasn't operating at a high level of awareness. Imagine parenting, guiding, and teaching your teenager by asking several smart questions, without a whiff of sarcasm or condescension, and having them come up with their own answers in their own wisdom. What if you could almost see their confidence in who they are and what they are capable of working out for themselves increasing with every answer they found in their hearts and minds?

I teach kids to meditate. Their parents often think it's a joke and say, "Are you kidding? My son who games all day like it's air just meditated—and he liked it?" It works, and kids want relief, so they do it. I challenge you to start your meditation practice with your teenager and keep on trying. Don't give up. You will see changes in your relationships to yourselves, respectively, and with each other.

Future Implications of Being Aware

Being aware beats being unaware! It always feels worse to look back and try to retrospectively plot out the things that you had no idea were taking place—thoughts that were never spoken, chances that weren't supposed to be taken, and choices made that were not safe—that you might have noticed if you had been more aware. Maybe you wouldn't have been able to prevent the inevitable—that's not your job anyway—but I see how easily one choice after another can add up to something big and catastrophic, spinning a family into crisis mode.

I think of it like the public service announcements for not texting while driving, in which they say, "It can wait." Whatever we are doing, whatever thoughts we are glued to, like truth, and whatever we are tempted to obsess over in place of what is really going on—those can wait. We must question our assumptions in order to seek awareness. We must notice when we get weak due to poor self-care, numbing out, stress, and overwhelming emotions, and we must wake up.

If you can fight hard against human nature to remain aware of what is and what is not happening with your teenager, you will have the opportunity to be more effective and more connected and to express more love than you ever have. The result is that we really did make the impact we wanted to make while they still were with us, and we fostered the kind of relationship that will keep us close as we grow older together. How do we do that if we are distracted with justifications and justified by our distractions?

Nice

Seems like a cute little word, compared to the rest, but please consider that a little "nice" goes a long way, like with hair gel.

It's the First Thing to Go

A kind tone, simple courtesies, thoughtfulness, mercy, generosity of spirit—call it what you want, but it is the first thing to go in families sometimes. We get so comfy that we get a little nasty at times. We let it all hang out, and it can breed a culture of rudeness, shortness, sarcasm, meanness, and insensitivity.

There's also fake nice—I'm not talking about that! No teeth grinding allowed!

It's Easy

What are some kind, positive statements that you have let go of mentioning to your teens, which, when they were younger, you were more vocal about?

Can you think of a time in the past week when someone, even a stranger, showed you an act of kindness, and it altered your experience of that moment?

Now, think about the meanness in the world. Sorry! You can stop! Let's consider that we can make a new habit of encouragement, of talking our kids up, and of looking for what they are doing right, as well as the tiny wins that they get in their life.

What are some areas of life in which you can make a point to encourage or acknowledge your teenager?

What can you say for each area that would make a difference, even if it seems like they are blowing it off?

You're So Embarrassing!

Have you ever started to say something negative about your kids in front of them to another person?

"Easton thought it would be a great idea to wash his red soccer socks with his white sheets today." (Wait! Easton's doing laundry? This is awesome! Bad example.)

How about if you said, "Jessie got an F on her quiz today. I'd told her to study, but she thought she had it all worked out." And then you roll your eyes.

I know it can seem casual or normal to disrespect our kids this way, but think about if your spouse or best friend were to disparage you in front of another person, using judgment or shame to fill someone in. It stings.

Teenagers tend to shut down, possibly after raging, instead of communicating immediately and effectively that their feelings were hurt. They often feel like it's a badge of honor to say, "I'm good. It's cool," when really they are embarrassed, ashamed, or not sure how to proceed; they need help and teaching.

Then, there we are, the ones whom the teens believe may be able to help, but because of our unkind, frustrated outburst, we take ourselves out of the running of safe places to go. We become one of the many judges from whom they must defend themselves. And our saying that we were kidding, or, "Well, it's true," does not undo the damage and shame that come with speaking negatively about someone to another.

I Judge Because I Care

Let's take *nice* from another angle. I may be in the minority, but as a retired judge of all things in the universe, I think that judgment is rooted in caring. If you didn't have an opinion or a "better" point of view, and if you weren't using your skills of analysis and logic to help a person see things in a more useful way, you wouldn't care at all—am I right?

Judgment or making a case for what is wrong with your teen or their choices is often more effective when encouragement runs the show.

I believe in straight talk. We are very direct and effective communicators in my family, and that is what I teach and promote for all of my clients also, but at the same time, tact and delivery are often underrated.

Just think of any time someone deals with you and goes straight to the *what's wrong* part of something that you worked hard on or were attempting to master. Acknowledging your effort and commenting on what's right about it—up until it didn't work and after—goes a long way to keep you listening and to have you become and remain open to that person's thoughts and ideas.

Why would we speak or act in anger—or even give off the vibe of being angry or disappointed—and still expect another person (especially one who is not fully mature and developed) to not pull into their turtle shell or throw up their fists when you want to get through to them? This is a valuable skill that we understand when it's applied to us, but it's very easy to forget that we need to use it ourselves if we want to be effective in helping someone see something our way.

Dog Poop Is Not Recyclable

Option 1: You say, "Geez! What the heck? I told you to get the dog poop from the side yard and to put it in the black trash can, not the recycle can! Why can't you do a simple thing? Do you really think dog shit is recyclable? I'll just do it myself. Don't bother." And then you sigh heavily.

Option 2: You say, "Hey, remember when I asked if you'd handle the dog poop yesterday? I noticed that you missed some in the side yard. What am I missing? Why didn't you do the whole job? And by the way, I think you made a mistake and put it in the recycle can. I know you care about the environment and everything, but I think you took it a little far." (You've shown humor and lightness and have given the benefit of the doubt.)

Maybe you'll find out your teen was upset about something and didn't mean to be so distracted or absentminded. Maybe you'll find out that they gag every time they have to clean up after the dog and would rather do *any* other chore than that one. Maybe they will appreciate your mercy and be nicer to their sibling (or even you) the next time there's a mistake or someone falls short.

Insults lead to kids deciding that you don't think much of them, that there must be something fundamentally wrong with them, and that they are somehow incapable. They shut down and stop trying. If they are going to get ripped up either way, why bother?

Yes, we get tired of saying the same things. Yes, we are right that they are wrong, but is it going to hurt us or them to use a kind tone? No. Do we have to deal with our own myriad frustrations and annoyances in life to be able to access a peaceful version of ourselves? Yes. Don't worry; I'll get to meditation again in a minute.

Don't Call Me Pollyanna

I am not a fan of babying people or beating around the bush, but I do apply those sayings that somehow usually apply to other people to teenagers too.

Here's one:

> In life you can never be too kind or too fair; everyone you meet is carrying a heavy load. When you go through your day expressing kindness and courtesy to all you meet, you leave behind a feeling of warmth and good cheer, and you help alleviate the burdens everyone is struggling with.
>
> —Brian Tracy

Do not gag. Think about what it would be like if your household operated, based on this quote alone—you know, if the kids treated the adults, the adults treated the kids, and the kids treated the kids (and even that awful dog) in a way that was kind, fair, courteous, warm, and cheerful. That might be kind of nice.

It only takes one person to bring the kindness and transform an entire household. Tomorrow, they can take the day off, as long as someone is focused on being nice, kind, and thoughtful, it can work.

Be the Change, or Forget about It

What would it be like to model the thing you want, instead of nagging or yelling about it?

We have to start connecting the dots and releasing entitlement mindsets, like, "They are my kids, and I'll speak to them with respect when they straighten up. And until then, they get to hear me yell about everything!"

Infusing kindness into our conversations, corrections, suggestions, or our little moments, in order to get the peace and the type of functional relationship that we want with our teens is something worth working on.

I do not think this is easy. It's not like anyone enjoys yelling at people or being snide or snippy. It's just that when our own wells of kindness are dried up, from where are we supposed to draw kindness for someone else, let alone that blasted teenager who is always hanging around?

Case 5 for Meditation

Robert Wright, author of *Why Buddhism Is True,* believes that meditation not only makes us happier, but it also makes us nicer, less selfish, and more considerate of others. He says, "I think the salvation of the world can be secured via the cultivation of calm, clear minds and the wisdom they allow" (https://blogs.scientificamerican.com/cross-check/can-meditation-make-us-nicer).

So if there's even a small chance that the salvation of the world could be wrapped up in meditation or prayer or Buddha or Jesus or being considerate of others or being less selfish—or just being nicer—then is there somewhere else you need to be?

Meditation is the weirdest, cheapest, most singularly powerfully peaceful weapon we have against all of the obstacles that we face in relating to and making a positive difference with our teenagers. That may hit you as absolutely ridiculous. Maybe you want it to be harder, much more strategic, or more power- or control-based. But what if it's true?

(Siri, find a yoga studio near me.)

Future Implications of Being Nice

Let's try this out with focus and intention for this one reason: to not to be hypocrites anymore as we yell down the hallway, *"Be nice to your brother!"*

The things that are true in life are true. Being nice matters. Kindness, gentleness—they matter. We must get a handle on whatever lies have us believing that we are weak or stupid when we choose kindness. The rhetoric that seeps into our subconscious about how teenagers are only nice when they want something is toxic. The idea that being nice is a way to manipulate is gross. Yes, of course that's true, but it's also true of cruelty and abuse. We must make a choice about which traits and behaviors we want to model in our homes.

Being nice and being naive are not the same thing. We know this, and even if you get played from time to time, you will at least know that you treated your teenager in the way you wish your parents had treated you, or with as much kindness as your parents showed you, if you had that kind of parents.

CLEAN Summary

You're aware of what makes you MEAN. You have a glimpse into the power of being REAL. Now you have CLEAN.

Being *c*onnected, *l*evelheaded, *e*xpressive, *a*ware, and *n*ice are absolutely the bridge between what you are feeling and dealing with in your home—with your teen, most likely, but even within yourself—and where you want to be; the vision that you have for your life, for your well-being, and for your future.

This is not an overnight thing. When you focus on being CLEAN, it's funny that all you will see is how dirty you are. That's how that works, but it's okay. You can meditate and see those lies for what they are. You won't be able to subsist on lies and self-abuse anymore with a clean conscience. You see now that there's a way to get what you want for you and your teenager without falling back on control, power plays, manipulation, or acting out of anger or frustration.

Game on. I challenge you to find ways to incorporate these ideas into practices and then develop those practices into mastery.

Part 4
What Is a Fully Functional Relationship?

What Does One Look Like, Sound Like, and Feel Like?

Here's the thing we all want and the thing people swear we can't have. It's the thing people say must be fake or must be because you're a pushover parent or some junk like that. Do you believe it is possible to be *all* you, full-out, holding nothing back, and allowing your teenager the space to do the same while you both interact and support each other?

Here's a what a fully functional relationship with your teen looks like, sounds like, and feels like:

Messiness and Imperfection—and It's Okay

Both parent and teen have space for each other to have a bad day or a sour reaction or to go through something huge and heavy—you know the stuff that is inevitable in life—and come through it with a closer bond. Both parent and teen are able to get what they need, not make sweeping decisions about the character of each other, based on judgment, fear, and protection or defensiveness. A cohesiveness is present—it's us against the world, not me against you or each against the world.

Respectfulness

Both parent and teen listen and care. They want to understand and learn from each other. The hierarchy setup is taken down, boundaries are honored, and mutual trust is present and experienced by both parties.

When parents have to make hard calls—the kind that only parents can do—if they employ 360-degree consideration, then even when the teen is upset and doesn't understand or like the call, the teen can maintain a level of respect toward the parent. Also, the parent does not lord their power over the teenager.

Cooperation

Cooperation looks like operating as a team, working together, and helping each other, with both giving and both taking. The vibe is balanced, fun, and productive; it's able to graciously pick up the slack for each other in difficult times, knowing that neither is being taken advantage of or feeling obligated to show up as awesome for the other. I know the F-word is something people preach passionately against in parenting, but I think a type of cooperation is like being a *friend* to your teenager—the best kind of friend they've ever had. Cooperation, support, and friendship, modeled in the flesh by a parent to a child, is a miraculous thing.

Fun

Fun sounds like laughter, dancing in the kitchen, making time to play and get into stuff together, sending fun messages and texts, popping in on each other, sharing developments and thoughts, cooking, eating, singing with the music way up in the car, and sharing inside jokes, games, and heated competitions. This is the kind of environment in which people don't have to make a big deal out of nothing, and when people want to make nothing much into a big deal, like a movie night, everyone is on board. At the same time, no one is obligated to be fun or have fun that is not authentic, and they don't get pressured to "cheer up."

Open-Mindedness

Being open-minded means you end up learning and growing because your kid is so smart. You can stop needing to be the be-all and end-all of the relationship, the almighty parent. You model being flexible and trying new ways of thinking and doing things. They end up trying some things that you think of too. You get a sense of relief and freedom and pride in yourself for changing, adapting, and innovating. So do they.

Happiness/Ease

Mornings, school, grades, logistics, chores, practicing sports and music, going to family events, getting teens to answer your phone or text, curfews, conversations, stressful news, spending time at the dinner table—all of that stops being an opportunity for your teenager to show you that you aren't going to win. They won't have to make their point to not please you by making your life more difficult at each turn. It's *easier.* The power struggles were never about laundry and math homework, but you can see that now. Can't you?

Influence

All those things you've been storing up to tell your kids someday when they become old enough—all those lessons and pieces of wisdom and advice, the stuff you want them to remember you for when you're gone and teach their own kids—can get through to them at a heart-level now. They will be receptive. Why?

Because you can get out of your head and your stubborn beliefs. You can stop seeking control and dominance, stop coming from fear, and *truly* understand and have compassion for what it's like to be them. You will have the keys to the kingdom! You will have their trust. You will be someone they admire and really seek input from. Can you even imagine it?

Your teens are entering the world soon. Will they still talk to you after they leave? Will they come back by choice? Will they want to answer your texts, calls, and emails? Will they dread coming home for the holidays? Will they want you to visit their dorm or their home?

Will you still get to share life with them? Will you get to be in your grandchildren's lives? Will they turn to you when things get hard and not just to ask for money? Will you be able to enjoy the fruits of your labor?

In a fully functional relationship between a parent and a teenager (future adult), there is a beautiful opportunity for continuity and freedom to pursue a different kind of relationship of choice, rather than the dependence or obligation that childhood requires. You can have this. You can.

I hate to be dramatic, but it needs to be said—and more often too. We do not know when our time is up. We *must* get our shit together as soon as possible because we do not have a certain future—and neither do our children.

Part 5
Overview of the Course: From MEAN to REAL CLEAN: How to Create a Fully Functional Relationship in Five Steps

If You're in the Course or Thinking about It, Read On

It's go time. By the end of my course, you will be able to predict what your kid will say about you at your funeral someday (hopefully, *extremely* far into the future). I'm being a little bit silly, but think about it: what if you could live like you were on a mission—not a high-pressure, stressful one but a challenging and rewarding mission to actually be the type of happy, healthy, humble, loving, responsible, intentional, trusted person you would wish your teen to be?

We will start the tactical work that is tangible to create accomplishments for you that support that you are actually operating in a REAL, CLEAN way.

This is going to be hard, but if relating to and raising your teen was easy, you wouldn't be here right now. You wouldn't expect your training to climb Mount Everest to be easy. You wouldn't expect a course on organic chemistry to be simple. If something doesn't occur as a challenge, and you don't have to push yourself (or let someone awesome like me push you), then you probably won't grow or change, and things will remain as they are but maybe with some cool new insights or books to read.

Not on my watch. You're with me on this, and my intention for this course is to set you on a new path. The end result is not coming from *magic*. It's from hard work and *action*.

You will have to do things, say things, and change things.

Wanna Fight at Base Camp or Get Climbing?

I have this picture in my head of a parent and a teen at the base of a hiking trail that leads up the steep, tall mountain. They stand at the bottom and bicker. They tell each other all the things they don't like and whatever they each fear, resent, and dread about the hike, each other, the weather—all of it.

"Why didn't you put ice in my water?"

"Why didn't *you* put ice in your water?"

"Why are you wearing that? God! You're so embarrassing."

"How could you forget to put on sunblock?"

"It doesn't matter. I doubt you'll make it to the top anyway."

"I do not want to hear you whine the whole way. Are you listening?"

"What if I get a blister? Why are we even here?"

You feel the vibe? How long will this go on before someone takes a step, with the parent as the leader, the one who's conquered plenty of mountains before? Right now, neither is walking; no one is ascending.

They may even get so tired from blaming and bickering that they go back home. There's nothing clean here. There's nothing real. It's just mean and nonfunctioning. No growing, no bonding, no forward motion.

New scene:

"Okay. Let's do this."

"I don't know how it's going to go exactly, but we can do this."

"Yes! We are strong, capable, prepared, and ready for anything, and no matter what, this is going to be really awesome—something we are really proud of."

"Let's take our before-pic and get going!"

"Okay, but I'm nervous. This is the longest hike I've ever done."

"Yeah, me too, but we've got this. I promise! Okay. Ready?"

"Ah! Okay! Yep!"

The mountain is *life*. The base is where you are now. If you want to be positional, defensive, righteous, or judgmental toward yourself or me or my ideas, you certainly can be, but I am 100 percent positive that if you do what I'm saying and let me lead you so you can lead your teen up this mountain, you will get there.

You can't see the top yet. You may not think you can do this. You may be ready to compromise with yourself and settle for something less beautiful than you are capable of and ready for and that's far less functional than you want.

Here Are the First Five Steps of the Journey

(Then I'll let you go on from there without me.)

Step 1: At your age right now, regardless of the quality of the relationship you had with your parents, whether they are living or not, can you imagine opening up a letter to read their words that take you through year by year, scene by scene, and that admit mistakes and come clean for all of the things they wish they had done better? Did you know there's a very specific way to make things right with people?

You will write a letter like that to your teenager. It will alter the relationship forever, even if it's already pretty good. It will set you both on a new path.

Step 2: I'm going to teach you how to let yourself off the hook, to truly forgive yourself for anything and everything that has gone down, from present day back to when you were two years old. You, my friend, will be a clean slate, with all the wisdom and lessons from the hard knocks but with none of the pain and *misery that* comes from unforgiveness. This is worth $1,000,000,000. Contact me for a payment plan.

Step 3: Your REAL CLEAN Life Plan

I go into serious-mindset coaching mode here, and we leave no single stone unturned. We hunt like predators, sniffing and looking for each and every source of stress, pain, disorganization, overwhelming issues, negativity, and garbage in your life. We get your poop officially into a group. If you take this step as if your life depends on it, you can count on my process and my love and support to get you to a new level of operating in your life. I've helped so many people do this work, free from judgment, guilt, making anything you're doing or have done "wrong." This part is not for babies.

Step 4: Your REAL CLEAN Agreement

We go deep in setting up your life to be one large agreement with yourself, your teen, and your family about how you want to operate and deliver on your REAL CLEAN life plan

Step 5: Your REAL CLEAN Commitment

Finally, we make some promises. We create the vision and the words to perfectly articulate what you are about; what your teen and your family can count on you for; and how you want to go down in history. Ever think about what kind of legacy you will leave when you go? Let's not leave that to chance or assumption.

If you want to buy my course, you can share the cost with a group of parents. I feel you'd want to share it anyway, so now you can pitch it to them before you buy and split the investment.

Go to my website: www.vbakermindset.com.

You'll get a lot of extra support from me if you want to join the MEAN->REAL CLEAN private Facebook group for a small monthly fee.

(Siri, play "End of the Road" by Boyz II Men.)

If this is the end of the road for us, then right now, I want you to know how much I appreciate a few things:

1. You opened up a book about parenting teens and invested a few hours into reading it, which means not only do you care, but you are committed to a better outcome with your teenager than the one you were previously on track for. That's very cool of you. I honor you for that.

2. Thank you for trusting me to get into your business, to challenge you, and to make you a little bit angry and defensive at times. Thanks for sticking it out. Thanks for bringing your full self to these lessons. I expected nothing less.

3. Thank you for honoring my own vulnerability as I shared with you the hard things that I've experienced in my life. In this world of brave little trolls, I knew I wouldn't be totally safe in writing this book and sharing some of my life and ideas with you, but I know I'll be okay because if I helped you make even one small shift in your mindset about yourself and/or your teenager, then it was a good plan on my part.

Thank you for your support. Keep up with me on social media, where I'll share my heart out for your benefit.

I love you,
Vanessa Baker
v@vbakermindset.com

Made in the USA
Las Vegas, NV
03 February 2021